TALK LIKE A WINNER

TALK LIKE A WINNER

21 Rules for Communication Success

STEVE NAKAMOTO

JAICO PUBLISHING HOUSE

Ahmedabad Bangalore Chennai
Delhi Hyderabad Kolkata Mumbai

Published by Jaico Publishing House
A-2 Jash Chambers, 7-A Sir Phirozshah Mehta Road
Fort, Mumbai - 400 001
jaicopub@jaicobooks.com
www.jaicobooks.com

This translation published in arrangement with
Columbine Communications & Publications
Walnut Creek, California, USA
www.columbinecommunications.com

To be sold only in India, Bangladesh, Bhutan,
Pakistan, Nepal, Sri Lanka and the Maldives.

TALK LIKE A WINNER
ISBN 978-93-88423-30-4

First Jaico Impression: 2019
Second Jaico Impression: 2023

Printed by
Repro India Limited, Mumbai

This book is dedicated to all the men and women who strive to be better everyday communicators so they can achieve the kind of success and happiness at work and in life that they know deep inside is rightfully theirs.

May these simple and powerful rules take you there.

You may not realize that it's no accident that you're reading this book. Evidently, you're ready to receive these messages of awareness in your life right now.

I guarantee that the journey you are about to take will be a lot easier and far more fun than you ever imagined.

All you really have to do is fall in love with the idea of you "talking like a winner" now! You don't have to force anything. It will all come to you naturally. That's because you already have these God-given abilities inside of yourself.

I'm only here to help you uncover them.

With Love & To Your Success,

Steve

Disclaimer

This book is designed to provide ideas and information on communication, relationships, and success. It is sold with the understanding that the publisher and author are not engaged in rendering professional services of any kind. If expert assistance is required, the services of a competent professional should be sought first and foremost.

Every effort has been made to make this book as complete and accurate as possible. However, there may be mistakes, both in typography and in content. Therefore, this text should be used only as a general guide for exploring ideas, and not as the ultimate source of communication, personal development, or psychological information.

The stories set forth in this book, while based in part on fact, have been modified so as not to reveal the identity of any real person. Any resemblance between persons depicted in this book and real persons is strictly coincidental.

The purpose of this book is to enlighten, inspire, and entertain the reader. The author and publisher shall have neither liability nor responsibility to any persons or entity with respect to any loss or damage caused or alleged to be caused directly or indirectly by the information, ideas, and suggested assignments presented in this book.

If you do not wish to be bound by the statements above, you are entitled to return this book directly to the publisher, Java Books, for an immediate product refund.

Contents

Introduction

This is a book about "*private* speaking" as opposed to "*public* speaking." By *private* speaking, I mean the effective use of everyday conversational skills. For most people, *private* speaking does not sound like a very sexy or important topic. After all, doesn't everyone know how to talk effectively in private with friends, family members, co-workers, and business associates? On the other hand, a person who achieves excellence in *public* speaking appears to possess a natural talent that can be a huge asset for personal and professional success.

But through my own experiences, I've discovered that it is *private* speaking and <u>not</u> *public* speaking which is the real secret to achieving your own potential for success and happiness. It's the ability to interact on a personal level through effective *private* speaking that sets free the power and beauty that lies within each one of us for the whole world to enjoy, appreciate, and respect.

And in a strange twist of fate, it seems that the better you become at *private* speaking, the easier it becomes for you to develop effective *public* speaking and self-confidence as well. In this Introduction, you'll discover how I came to know that this statement is true.

The Big Secret I Locked Deep Inside

For most of my life, I've had a terrible fear of public speaking. I remember one regrettable time when I gave an oral report in my 7th grade English class and I started shaking and gasping for air. Unable to finish my report, I stopped and faced my class while Mr. Heilman, my cold-hearted English teacher, criticized me at great length for my embarrassingly poor performance.

I soon developed an intense phobic response to situations where I would have to speak up in front of other people. Somehow I was able to slip through high school and college by making excuses, missing assignments, and dropping classes that required me to make speeches, give oral reports, or read aloud to the class.

One of the few times that I actually had to confront this fear in my adult life was when I gave the world's shortest wedding toast as my friend's best man. The toast that I presented went something like: "Congratulations to a wonderful couple, Kurt and Linda. What more can I say?"

By the time I reached my early 30s, I had resigned myself to a life in which I'd keep this secret speaking phobia concealed forever.

Finding The Courage To Change

A lot was going on in my early 30s including moving to a new area, ending a longtime love relationship, and being involved in a near-fatal car crash. Shortly after the accident, a friend told me that I had to go see a guy named Tony Robbins speak. This friend described Mr. Robbins as a young, up-and-coming self-help guru who might one day become the President of the United States. (Note: At this point in time, Anthony Robbins has not fulfilled my friend's expectation of becoming the President of the United States. But Mr. Robbins has made a name for himself as the #1 peak performance expert and highest-paid motivational speaker in the world. That's still very impressive indeed!)

To make a long story short, I went to see Tony Robbins speak, signed up for his weekend seminar, and learned, amongst other things, about therapeutic techniques for overcoming fears. I gradually became more involved in his entire assortment of personal development programs and at one of his more intimate workshops I stood up in front of a hundred people to reveal my speaking fear. As expected, I started to shake, heard my voice crack, and was having difficulty breathing.

But despite this public embarrassment, I had clearly created a defining moment in my life! It was the first time that my courage to succeed actually exceeded my fear of humiliation. And while the therapeutic techniques from the Tony Robbins seminars did not instantly end my speaking fears, I felt that somehow my courage and commitment would eventually help me find a way to finally solve my lifelong speaking challenges.

GETTING STUCK ON THE ROAD TO RECOVERY

For the next few years, I attended various classes and seminars in the area of communications, personal development, and leadership. Some of these classes were quite elementary for me, like those that taught people how to talk to anyone or get others to like you. On the other hand, the advanced communication courses – such as those in the fields of hypnosis and unconscious persuasion – seemed manipulative and too unnatural to perform. Despite the claims made by the advanced communication courses, I found that these types of trainings were more likely to make a person come across as being some sort of weirdo than as a confident, likeable person that people outside of the seminar world would actually trust.

At this point in my road to recovery, I had essentially run out of self-improvement classes to take in order to overcome my speaking challenges. Despite my major investments in time, money, and effort, I still felt deep inside that I had made only minor progress in my overall communication effectiveness and self-confidence.

WHAT MY FRENCH SKI INSTRUCTOR TOLD ME

One sport that I enjoy but have never been much good at is snow skiing. I was a very competent ocean surfer in my youth, but snow skiing on big scary mountains presented a new kind of athletic challenge for me. So I took up skiing in my adult years with the full intention of becoming skilled at it by taking lots of expensive group lessons.

After a few years of these lessons, I found myself at the Copper Mountain Club Med Resort in Colorado taking one week of intensive ski instructions. During those seven days at Copper Mountain, my French ski instructor spent a lot of time showing me different techniques and sharing his philosophy about mastering the sport of skiing. He eventually told me something that would change my life forever and it wasn't just about skiing. What he said was this:

"Steve, I can't show you any more techniques. If you want to get better, you're just going to have to ski more miles."

What this meant to me was that I needed to get lots of practice doing a variety of simple skills so that I'd have a solid foundation in skiing to build from. And relating this to my speaking ability, I also didn't need a lot of expensive seminars or advanced communication techniques in order to become more confident and effective. What I needed was a lot of practice doing the fundamentals well.

MY PRACTICE FIELD: TOUR DIRECTING

During the first week of January 1992, I saw an advertisement in the *Los Angeles Times* Sunday Travel Section that read: *Get Paid to Travel.* The ad intrigued me. Soon I was at an introductory meeting hearing about becoming a certified professional tour director. I learned that after getting the certification, I could lead groups, travel the world, and get paid while doing so.

Despite a variety of interesting career options at the time, I chose to pursue the tour director profession because it presented me with a low-pressure opportunity to practice and refine my communication skills. Essentially, tour directing offered me up to eight hours a day of public speaking experience involving a variety of topics, situations, and ever-changing audiences.

My first assignments as a tour director were with 35 or more British and Australian tourists on 14-day sightseeing tours across the Western United States and Canada. In my role as a tour director, I had to relate well to a large number of people from different cultures about topics that I didn't know a whole lot about such as history, government, geology, and horticulture. It was also expected of me to be friendly and professional while I was leading a tour. Otherwise I'd receive poor evaluations from the tour passengers that could result in getting fired from my job.

Quite frankly, I wasn't very good at tour directing at first. But by the third year of my tour directing career, I was getting to be very comfortable and effective as an all-around communicator and group travel leader.

MY TESTING GROUND: 220 PLUS RADIO INTERVIEWS

In 2000, I wrote a book titled *Men Are Like Fish: What Every Woman Needs To Know About Catching A Man.* This book idea came from a combination of my experiences in the dating world, an understanding of the use of metaphors as a tool for learning, and my lifelong love for the sport of fishing.

In this book, I made a detailed analogy of how catching a man from a woman's perspective is a lot like how a fisherman catches a fish. Essentially in the sport of fishing, an angler must know what kind of fish they want to catch, use the right bait to attract, create a secure attachment with the sharp hook, and skillfully reel their catch securely into the net. In a similar way, a woman seeking to "catch" the love of a man must know what type of man she wants to catch, be able to attract his undivided attention, create a strong emotional attachment, and skillfully secure his commitment to her.

With an intriguing title like *Men Are Like Fish,* it was easy for me to find radio stations that wanted to have me as a guest expert on their morning and afternoon drive-time talk shows. Usually, these radio shows wanted me on for a 10-15 minute segment in order to entertain their audiences about amusing ways that men can be "caught" in a romantic sense by women "anglers."

Promoting my book by going on radio talk shows was a real-time test of my newly developed speaking skills. While tour directing had given me the freedom and practice to express myself over an eight-hour period, being a guest on a drive-time radio show required me to be engaging, interesting, and concise under the pressure of performing before live radio audiences that numbered in the thousands.

With the high cost of airtime, a guest has to be instantly effective or else they are quickly cut off by the radio host or program manager. For example, Jay Thomas, a popular radio talk-show host who was then airing in New York City, pulled the plug on me after only two minutes on the air! Evidently, he didn't like my responses to his dating questions at all and thought I was being flippant with my seemingly endless assortment of fishing analogies.

But I learned from both my successes and failures like the one I experienced on Jay Thomas's radio show in New York. Perhaps the biggest lesson I learned was that in communication of any kind, it's not how much you know that matters. What does matter is *how well you connect with your audience.* Whether you're speaking to a large audience on a radio show in New York City or to just one person at work, it's creating an emotional connection with your audience that makes a conversation successful.

MY UNIQUE PERSPECTIVE: BECOMING MR. ANSWER MAN

Over a span of three years, I successfully appeared on over 220 radio and television talk shows promoting my *Men Are Like Fish* theme. I eventually drew the attention of *iVillage.com,* the largest online women's community in the world, and they eventually hired me to fill the role of the "Mr. Answer Man" relationship advisor. What I do is handle questions from women around the world (as many as 75 a day) and help them figure out the men in their love lives from an honest male perspective.

Over the years, I've become a sort of male "Dear Abby." In giving advice, I focus on being consistently understanding, kind-spirited, and helpful. As a result of being "Mr. Answer Man" for four-plus years, I've probably heard more real-life problems about romantic relationships on a day-to-day basis than just about any other man in America.

In January 2007, after reading and responding to a long series of relationship questions for *iVillage.com,* an idea dawned on me. Suddenly I could clearly see that *a large number of problems that people have with others boil down to challenges in the area of basic communications.* That's when I decided to begin work on a manuscript addressing the many facets of everyday communication. Eventually it evolved into this book, *Talk Like A Winner!*

WHAT WAS MISSING ON THE BOOKSHELF?

I felt that there were enough beginning books on communication that are targeted for those who have high-levels of fear or social awkwardness. And I also thought that there were enough advanced titles about persuasion power and unconscious rapport for professional salespeople or those in high positions of leadership. But what I believe was sorely missing is *the intermediate course on communication* that bridges the enormous gap between the novice and the expert.

Like in the sport of skiing, the overwhelming majority of the public is stuck at the intermediate level of skill. These are the people who are good enough to get by in life, but aren't bad enough to think that they need any help. In fact, most people believe that it's other people who need help in the area of communications and rarely is the responsibility for relationship problems put upon themselves.

This book is written for those individuals who aspire to greatness in their communication skills, interpersonal relationships, and achievements in life. It's for someone who realizes that *average skills equate to only average results at best, but greatness is reserved for those who work hard and smart at mastering the critical skills in life.*

HOW EXACTLY DO YOU IMPROVE YOUR COMMUNICATIONS?

In over 18 years of study, practice, and testing, I've concluded that most people believe that their primary responsibility in personal communication is talking. The largely overlooked and underappreciated areas of everyday communication are such things as: (1) listening to others while they speak, (2) evaluating the meaning of the message, and (3) responding in an enlightened manner, to name a few.

On closer examination, I've identified *21 key ingredients for effective personal communication* that I call "simple rules." They are simple because I've reduced the ingredient down to a single familiar action word such as "choose," "impact," "ask," and "reflect." While these rules may appear simple, they are also powerful because they can dramatically improve your conversational skills. And I call these items "rules" because if you violate the principle that they describe, you're likely to be punished in your life with consistently poor results.

At the same time, I believe that there's one basic reason why most people don't achieve more consistent success in their everyday communications. In effect, they don't know precisely what to do or at what stage in their conversations to perform these actions. In addition, people rarely practice and test what they need to do on a daily basis. As a result, they never develop higher skills in effective communications.

WHAT'S THE BIG DEAL IF I DON'T COMMUNICATE WELL?

A wise teacher once shared the following important insight with me. He told me that human unhappiness stems from the unsettling knowledge that a person is less than what they know they should be. It's like going to your final resting place with your gifts of life still unwrapped, unused, and unappreciated within yourself.

Believe me, I know what that feels like. My speaking fears made me more cynical and withdrawn than I knew I was deep inside. My inner misery had been covered up by years of hiding from my fears. But what was worse is that I was resigned to spending the rest of my life with the feeling that I was less than I was capable of being.

I sincerely hope that you see the strong connection between mastering your everyday communications and becoming a happier and more winning individual. Don't rip yourself off by simply letting things slide and settling for a mediocre life at best!

Since you picked up this book, I suspect that there's more to you as a person than what the world is presently seeing. But what *I* think isn't really important. What's important is that *you* know deep inside that there's a lot more to you than what you're currently living and that *you* are the one who can do something about it.

THE MASTER RULE: YOU MUST DESIGN YOUR OWN FUTURE!

There are two kinds of people in life. There are the winners and there are the losers. Losers always take the easy route in life and inevitably let their dreams and aspirations fade away over time. The loser's excuse for poor results in life is almost always that success and happiness just weren't in the cards for them.

Winners, on the other hand, take charge of their own life. They are willing to accept the pain of short-term setbacks in order to gain, achieve, or attract what they truly desire in their lives. But most of all, winners realize that in the grand scheme of life you have to accept both the credit and the blame for the person you eventually become.

Becoming a winner in life requires a clear decision by you. Are you willing to make a firm decision about how to design your desired future by working on enhancing your communication skills? I can tell you from experience that your efforts toward growth in the area will be deeply rewarded in the long run, with benefits also in the short run.

If your response to all of this is "I'm going to let this slide because it sounds like too much of a hassle," then I wish you good luck. Yes, luck is exactly what your future will have to rely on exclusively if that's your answer. But if you've decided on your own terms that this is the right time and place for action to improve your conversational abilities, then I say "Congratulations!"

Plus, I also want to leave you with these thoughts...

I am deeply honored by your decision to read this book. I promise to give you the best of what I've got so that it's worth your investment in both time and money. And I thank you for allowing me the privilege to share my experiences with you and a chance to make a difference in your life.

Let's do this process together and create a life for you that is simply magical! If you commit now to working with the steps in this book in the spirit of playful adventure, you too will soon be talking like a winner!

Here's to our magnificent journey together!

Steve Nakamoto
Huntington Beach, California
February 2008

How To Use This Book

Talk Like A Winner is packed with concentrated ideas and information and this could easily cause some readers to feel intimidated or overwhelmed. So it's important that you approach this book in a manner that fits your own time constraints, individual needs, and preferred learning style.

My intention is to help you *get the most information in the best way possible* so that you can change your life for the better. But in order to accomplish this objective, I need to help you find the approach that will suit *you* best.

With this in mind, I suggest the following ideas...

Some of you may choose to move right through the book quickly, skimming over what you already know and coming back to whatever interests you the most. This is the quickest and easiest way for people who already possess a solid foundation on this subject and who want to find and fix their own particular communication blind spots.

There will be others of you who will find it most useful to work on a chapter a week in a more thorough but gradual step-by-step learning process. This is the pace that I strongly suggest for people who want to make big changes happen in their communication style by putting in the necessary consistent hard work.

And there will be some readers who will prefer to simply pick a specific page or idea to focus on for a particular moment or specific need in their life. This option will work well as long as you remember to keep this book in a handy place so that you can refer to it quickly and often.

EXPRESS
LISTEN
ALIGN
RESPOND

TALK LIKE A *Winner!*

21 Simple Rules for Achieving Everyday Communication Success

PEOPLE ARE MY GREATEST RESOURCE

One

Think

OPERATE FROM AN ENLIGHTENED MINDSET

"The mind is more vulnerable than the stomach because it can be poisoned without feeling immediate pain."

Helen MacInnes
Author of *Assignment in Brittany* (1942)

think: 1. to reason about, ponder, or formulate in the mind. 2. to mentally process information, ideas, or concepts in order to effectively reach sought outcomes and internal desires. 3. as it applies to this book, the first level at which you need to organize in order to achieve everyday communication success and the ultimate goal of establishing and developing outstanding interpersonal relationships.

You're One Step Closer To Unleashing The Winner Within! *We all have a natural tendency to treat our daily conversations with a great degree of casualness. One of your main objectives as a master communicator is to take a more serious look at both the positive and negative consequences of the way we interact with others. That way, you can empower yourself with the right kind of thinking that will guide you naturally toward building better personal and professional relationships through smarter and more effective communication habits.*

Many of today's top Lexus and Acura luxury car models come factory-equipped with sophisticated voice-activated navigation systems. After prompting the system with a voice command, the input of an address, or in some cases even a telephone number, a driver of one of these vehicles can be guided with precise accuracy throughout most of the United States and major Canadian cities.

This means that you no longer have to be a skilled map-reader in order to arrive at your desired destinations even when you're in unfamiliar cities. With these modern navigation systems, you dramatically reduce the risk of getting lost and wasting precious time during personal trips around your hometown or when on your way to important business appointments.

Whether you're driving a new Lexus or Acura automobile or trying to achieve something of value in your life, it's important to have a reliable guidance system to help you get from where you are now to where you want to be in the future. Wandering around aimlessly without direction can be a frustrating and wasteful use of your time and energy in any field of endeavor.

Thinking Steers Your Vehicle In Life

Things that are produced inside the human brain, such as thoughts, ideas, and information forms, make up our personal mindset. This mindset influences our habits and behaviors, and it's the major determining factor in how our lives turn out.

> "Thinking is a soundless dialogue, it is the weaving of patterns, it is a search for meaning. The activity of thought contributes to and shapes all that is specifically human."
>
> Vera John-Steiner
> Author of *Notebooks of the Mind* (1985)

Our mindset comes from our references in life. These references are usually formed through our personal experiences, but are also influenced by our role models, peer groups, and media biases, as well as our formal and informal education. But sometimes we unwisely operate from outdated, distorted, or destructive references.

For example, most – if not all – of the things that happened to us while we were in elementary school are no longer relevant today. I remember having crooked teeth and a bad haircut in 2nd grade. Some of my obnoxious classmates poked fun at me by nicknaming me "White Fang" after a cartoon puppet that was popular at the time. Their hurtful act caused me to retaliate by calling other people unflattering nicknames as well. This destructive behavior on my part persisted well into my adult life until someone brought to my attention how these unflattering (but hilarious as heck!) nicknames were upsetting other people. Naturally, this was hurting my chances for developing better relationships with the friends and colleagues who I was making fun of behind their backs.

William James, the prominent American philosopher and psychologist (1842-1910) wrote, "The greatest discovery of my generation is that human beings can alter their lives by altering their attitudes of mind." In our own lives, the smart way to achieve goals and desires is to start first by using this insight from James and looking at possible changes in our mental attitudes.

If one of your goals is to establish or improve relationships through better everyday communication, then there are certain ways of thinking that will make this possible. The first step is to *get rid of destructive habits* like giving people unflattering nicknames! The second step is to *install empowering habits* that will naturally guide your actions towards building better relationships with others.

People Are Your Greatest Asset

A good starting place for acquiring the right mindset for communication success is to fully appreciate the value that other people can provide to you in terms of their examples of excellence or warnings of ineffectiveness. If we use our sense of awareness properly, we can emulate all of the effective communication habits that people in our lives have and at the same time avoid doing what doesn't appear to work well for them or others as well.

If you choose to do this, the finest examples of communication excellence can become your role models for more accelerated learning. These role models represent living, breathing 3-dimensional examples of people who can inspire you with real images of what great communication looks, sounds, and feels like in action.

For instance, an enlightened woman may choose to emulate people like actress Angelina Jolie, talk show host Oprah Winfrey, Senator Hillary Clinton, comedian/talk show host Ellen DeGeneres, news anchor Katie Couric, and/or actress Julia Roberts as real live role models in the area of effective communication. With increased awareness, a smart woman can pick up a lot of helpful pointers that she can implement into her own manner of interacting with others.

As for men, good male role models for effective communication might include people like late-night talk show hosts Jay Leno and David Letterman, ex-President Bill Clinton, television sports broadcaster Bob Costas, stock market advisor Jim "Mad Money" Cramer, television psychologist Dr. Phil

McGraw, Senator Barack Obama, or millionaire tycoon Donald Trump, to name a few. These are men who communicate effectively with clarity and passion, conveying messages that impact listeners in a powerful way.

When you realize the gift that other people provide you through their examples of excellence or their warnings of ineffectiveness, you'll begin embracing the opportunity to interact with more anticipation. In the end, it is your burning desire to interact well with a wide variety of people that will become one of your most important assets in accelerating your learning curve relating to mastering your communications and building outstanding relationships that last.

RULE #1: OPERATE FROM AN ENLIGHTENED MINDSET

Let's take a look at some constructive ways to think that will help you in your quest for successful everyday communications and improved relationships. Some of these ideas may already be a part of your personal mindset and will serve as a confirmation of wise thinking. But other items here may be something for you to seriously consider adopting into your new enlightened mindset.

- **If you have the will, then you'll find a way.** This attitude or belief is more than just an old English saying. It's also the driving force behind your success in any new endeavor. We all have things in our lives that we'd like to have, do, or become. But in order to attract or achieve those final outcomes, a person must acquire and maintain the burning desire to attain them. In regards to your desire to achieve everyday communication success and receive all of the benefits that this ability provides, you must really want this to happen for you. If your desire is weak, then you'll probably give up at the first sign of failure. But if you have the iron will to succeed, then you *must* find a way to make it happen. The bottom line is that it's not your problem to know exactly how to master your communications at any point in the process. The real thing that you need to do is turn up the heat of your desire and hold the belief that if you have the will to succeed, you'll find a way. Know deep within yourself that failure cannot win in the end when it's pitted against absolute persistence.

All relationships present opportunities. We all agree that great relationships with other people have multiple benefits including a chance to share ideas freely during conversations. But even interactions involving those we hardly know or with difficult individuals can be looked at as potential learning experiences. With folks who we encounter superficially in our daily lives, it's a chance to work on developing friendlier habits. And for people who we don't especially like to be around, a conversation is a chance to become a better listener, see things from their point-of-view, or to respond in a more understanding fashion. When you realize that all interactions with people present opportunities to practice your skills and test your character, then you'll be on your way to more rapid improvement in your communications.

People can open unseen doors for you. You never know who might say good things about you and who they could be chatting with during these conversations. If you develop a reputation as a friendly person of great value, then your stock will rise through word-of-mouth. That will result in other people wanting to meet you, becoming friends, and even introducing you to others in their circle of influence. Realize that people will do this naturally without your prior knowledge or conscious efforts.

Some relationships may come back to haunt you. When we treat other people carelessly or unfairly, we can leave them with resentment towards us. And while this may only result in having nothing to do with each other, it also means that you won't likely get any favors from them in the future either. Worse yet, some people may even go out of their way to say bad things about you behind your back and as a result close the door on potential opportunities. My father always told me to be kind to other people when they need you because you never know when the tables may be turned years later and you're the one who needs a favor from that other person. Keep this idea in mind before you feel tempted to say any unkind or unflattering words to someone. It's also important to remember when considering leaving someone out of your life.

One bad exchange can destroy a relationship forever. While it may take a number of conversations to convince another person of your friendship, always remember that it only takes one bad experience to end it. I remember a time when I unwisely accused my older brother of being a liar in front of some of his business colleagues. That embarrassing moment for my brother was enough to ruin our relationship for good. It's been several years since the two of us have had any meaningful interactions. Unfortunately, I learned a painful lesson the hard way by making careless, insensitive remarks in an important situation. I have done a lot of hard work since that time to improve the way I relate to other people.

Build your relationships one conversation at a time. While we may have presumptions about people before we meet them, a relationship is more largely shaped by actual conversations and personal interactions. Or you could overhear a person's conversation with other people and develop your initial impressions from that. But after a series of constructive interactions with another person, you may naturally start to develop rapport in a variety of areas. So you can see that, like a layer of building bricks, a solid relationship can be constructed one piece or enjoyable interaction at a time.

You never know what people will remember. I went to a professional volleyball tournament last summer in my hometown of Huntington Beach, California. I had a chance during a break in the action to chat with a famous retired pro player who was conducting a small clinic for spectators wanting to improve their own volleyball technique. After receiving a few pointers on how to hit the ball properly, I thanked the ex-pro player for his time and input. But what I remember most from our interaction was that he didn't reply to me by saying either *"You're welcome"* or *"It was my pleasure."* Instead, he simply turned and walked away from me. I know that the ex-pro player wasn't consciously trying to be rude to me, but I still felt a bit slighted in this memorable little incident. While it may not have mattered much to him, my guess is that this former player had no idea that he left that particular negative impression on a spectator like me.

- **Great relationships are the real pot of gold in life.** In our quest for personal achievement, it's always good to stop and remember the importance of quality relationships in the overall scheme of things. Life is nothing but a shallow existence without having other people sharing in the joy of your journey. While unhealthy relationships can create difficult challenges in your life, it shouldn't keep you from realizing that it's the good ones that make living more enjoyable and rewarding. In the end, it's not so much the money you've earned or the awards that you've achieved that matters, it's who you got to share your moments of joy with that really counts.

Most of all, remember that everyday communication has the potential to create big results over time in your life. When you approach each conversation with respect for the other people involved and appreciation for the moment at hand, you'll be taking a major step in the right direction toward successful everyday communication and improved personal and professional relationships.

PREPARE FOR YOUR NEXT CONVERSATION NOW!

Take a moment and look over the eight ideas for improving your communication mindset. From this list, select one item which you've understood clearly and used successfully in a positive way in your own life. In a short paragraph or two, write down a specific incident that you can refer to as an example of how operating from the correct mindset was constructive in developing or improving an important relationship of yours.

Now think of another situation that will likely come up in the next few days where operating from the right mindset will keep you guided towards a successful and more enjoyable interaction with another person. What is the one key reminder that you'll promise to keep in the front of your mind before this next important conversation? Write down the answer to this last question now while it's fresh in your mind and remember to refer to it right before that next important interaction.

The important point to remember here is that the way you think and the beliefs or attitudes that you hold to be true will automatically shape your destiny in life. If you can maintain an empowering mindset throughout your life with ideas like I've offered you in this chapter, you will naturally guide yourself in the direction of success and happiness. In the final analysis, it's not the circumstances of your life that matter most but how you evaluate and respond to whatever is happening at any given moment.

THE BOTTOM LINE

Remember that in order to "talk like a winner" in the broadest sense, you must "think like a winner" as well. All you have to do is follow a simple and powerful rule: *Operate from an enlightened mindset.* Once you appreciate the significance of this essential part of successful communication, it's only a matter of playing around with the ideas, practicing with a greater sense of purpose, and putting it to the test regularly in your own life until it becomes an automatic habit. It will be a lot easier than you ever imagined.

REMEMBER TO PRACTICE WITH PURPOSE
HOW TO LISTEN
TALK LIKE A WINNER

Two

Learn

STRETCH YOUR COMMUNICATION RANGE

"That is what learning is.
You suddenly understand something
you've understood all your life,
but in a new way."

Doris Lessing
Author of *The Four-Gated City* (1969)

learn: 1. to gain mastery through serious study and disciplined practice. 2. to acquire knowledge, attitudes, skills, or strategies through study, instruction, or experience that causes a change of behavior that is persistent, measurable, and specific. 3. as it applies to this book, how you can become more flexible and effective regardless of the situation by mastering a wider range of communication styles.

You're Another Step Closer To Unleashing The Winner Within!
Limited communication skills will limit the size of your audience and the variety of situations that you can perform in well. One of your primary objectives as a master communicator is to stretch yourself by learning a variety of new ways to communicate with others. That way, you'll be prepared to connect well with any person that you meet in your personal and professional life.

In its fifth and most widely-watched season, the popular musical talent show, *American Idol*, drew over 200 million viewers around the world for its two-hour final episode. In the end, Taylor Hicks, a 29-year-old Southern-style rhythm and blues singer from Alabama won a decisive victory over California's Katharine McPhee to be crowned that season's new *American Idol*.

While the show was once ridiculed as an over-hyped karaoke contest, the singing it features has evolved over the years into a more adventurous and stylistically diverse musical display. Some weeks of the competition involving Taylor Hicks presented musical themes centered around Motown,

Rock, Broadway, Big Band, and Country in order to showcase the versatility of each contestant's talents. Exposing glaring weaknesses in any musical genre opened up the strong possibility of being eliminated from the competition.

The winner of that season's *American Idol* show was ultimately the person who captured the greater share of the over 63 million votes (That's more than any American president has ever received!) which were cast during that final week. Taylor Hicks accomplished this by displaying a winning combination of musical diversity, charismatic showmanship, and personal likeability over the course of the entire multi-week singing competition.

Whether you're a contestant on the *American Idol* show or an average person talking with other people, the ability to communicate confidently in a variety of styles will make you more appealing to a wider audience. Developing new ways to interact with others through the work of this book will help you reach a greater number of people and allow you to feel more comfortable in a wider range of situations.

Challenge Your Comfort Level

The difference between your present ability to perform a task and your performance in the future can be bridged through learning. As long as you stay committed to excellence, stretch yourself with new challenges, and find enjoyment in the process, you'll eventually *learn your way* toward more success in whatever field you choose.

In your quest for everyday communication success, there are many areas to master. As noted above, one of the key areas is in developing the flexibility to communicate effectively in a variety of styles. Unfortunately, most people possess only a limited communication range and therefore have just a small array of people who they can connect with well.

During my early years as a tour director, I had to learn how to communicate effectively with a variety of different people and age groups. Many tours that I lead were comprised of visitors to the U.S. including people from such countries as Great Britain, Australia, South Africa, Canada, and Israel. I also had to lead tour groups comprised of American clients including high school students, church members, college alumni, senior citizens, and business people.

Each group presented their own unique challenge in my effort to be a winning tour guide. For example, I had to be "cool and hip" with the high school kids, but professional and articulate with the business groups. With senior citizens, I had to be more mature in how I related, while foreigners really wanted to feel a sense of deep passion from me about sharing the wonders of our country with them.

One time, a church group from Los Angeles complained to the tour company that I was working for then about my inappropriate sense of humor and almost got me fired. In another instance, a group from San Antonio, Texas gave me almost no money in customary gratuities because they thought that I didn't care about them. In both cases, my ineffectiveness in relating personally to these people resulted in immediate negative feedback which, frankly, hurt my feelings. But I learned a lot by being thrown into the fire with these challenges, particularly about how it takes extra awareness and skill to broaden one's communication horizons.

Today, the progress that I made during my tour guiding days has helped me become more effective in my professional life as an author and speaker, and also a better communicator in my personal life. All that it's taken is a willingness to stretch my comfort zone and face the possibility of short-term pain with the promise of eventually getting better over time.

Rule #2: Stretch Your Communication Range

Understand that your greatest progress will not come from doing what is quickest and easiest for you. In order to increase your abilities, you'll have to challenge yourself by doing what might seem uncomfortable at first.

The following suggestions are designed to help you develop a wider range of communication styles so that you'll be ready for almost any situation that comes your way:

- **Meet lots of different people.** Practice by conversing with everyone you meet. It could be with the cashier at the supermarket, people in line at the bank, someone at your doctor's office, a co-worker taking a coffee break, or a neighbor who is out walking their dog. How about trying a fun social activity like becoming a regular at a popular local eatery, joining a reading group, signing up for a guided tour of a local historic site, or taking a co-ed exercise class? Optimally, you'll want to meet people of different ages like kids and seniors, as well as people from other areas like foreign-born Americans or tourists from other states. The idea is to pick up lots of different speaking styles while you practice your own ability to communicate, overcome shyness, and build self-confidence.

@ **Talk less, listen more.** This may be the simplest communication tip to implement. Just changing the focus away from you and toward the other person will instantly and dramatically improve your overall communication effectiveness. While you're practicing this new discipline, you will most likely get better at listening as well as pick up subtle ways of doing a more effective job of speaking.

@ **Talk more if you're generally shy.** Shyness is one of those things that you just have to bite the bullet on and "get over it." We all have moments or environments where we don't feel entirely comfortable and speaking up isn't something that comes naturally. But when shyness becomes your standard way of dealing with people, it strictly limits the quantity and quality of your relationships. For starters, get yourself into small, low-pressure conversations. Talk about simple things in life that everyone notices. Some good examples might be: *"How bad is the traffic on your way to work?" "What do you think about this strange weather?"* and *"What about the outrageous price of gasoline?"* Say a few words like these and then let the other person have a chance to talk.

@ **Adjust your speed and volume for different effects.** There are times when being selective about what you cover regarding your topic and/or speaking more quickly have their advantages. For example, when you're telling a story, it's important to skip through the unnecessary details in order to get to your point before your audience begins to tune you out. You also want to put energy and excitement into your voice as well to show others that you're genuinely excited about what you're talking about. On the other hand, there are times when you want to slow down your rate of speaking to show thoughtfulness or emotion. Or you will want to speak slower in order to connect better with people who have a natural tendency to talk at a more leisurely pace. In addition, your volume and speed need to vary at times in order to avoid having a boring monotone while you're speaking.

Develop skill and self-confidence by telling jokes. An indirect way of improving your communication skills is by learning how to tell a good narrative joke. Offering jokes will teach you how to tell a story quickly, describe a situation with freshness, and deliver the punch line with a straight face. A couple things to remember about telling jokes are to make sure that you don't offend others with the content and to refrain from laughing at your own joke before it's finished. You might also buy or rent a DVD of your favorite comedian in order to see how professionals skillfully tell jokes and funny stories to entertain audiences. You might pick up a few helpful tips on developing your own style of tasteful humor just from watching the pros through repeated viewings.

Practice a more formal way of speaking. When I was 10 years old, my family moved to Palos Verdes, an upper middle-class suburb of Los Angeles. I immediately began to notice how well-spoken the kids were who lived there. I remember running into a classmate at a local restaurant one night who impressed the heck out of me when he smoothly introduced me to his parents by saying, *"Dad and Mom, I'd like you to meet my friend, Steve Nakamoto. Steve and I are in the same math class together. Steve, this is my father and* *mother."* By increasing your range into more formal areas, you'll have the style and skill to walk into a wider variety of social situations with more self-confidence and overall effectiveness.

- **Develop a more informal manner of speaking as well.** Be sure that you can touch people with a casual style of conversing as well. The 20-year-old guys that I play beach volleyball with often greet me by saying simply, *"Dude, what up?"* Their style of talking is quick and light. When these young guys talk, they're in, they're out, and then they're moving on. And they usually try to leave you laughing or smiling. That's not a bad way to conduct a conversation when you have lots of places to go and tons of people to interact with each day.

- **Study or mimic other people's styles.** The next time you turn on a television talk show, be sure to notice the way top-rated hosts communicate with their audiences. Whether you like to observe Jay Leno, Oprah Winfrey, David Letterman, Ellen DeGeneres, or Montel Williams, begin to notice their facial expressions, hand gestures, changes in voice tones, as well as how they listen, ask questions, give compliments, and tell stories. When you have highly-effective communicators to model, you can quickly accelerate your growth by paying close attention and picking up valuable pointers along the way.

Commit to stretching your abilities by stepping out of and eventually expanding your comfort zone and you'll be taking an active step in your learning process. Begin by paying attention to details and becoming more aware of how you can improve your communications. The next step is to create your own communication-expanding assignments so that you actually challenge yourself to do something in that direction. What you know intellectually will be of little or no value unless you take action while the ideas are fresh in your mind.

FIND JUST ONE TASK TO DO TODAY!

From the preceding list of suggestions, select one item that you can easily do today. Now find another item and make it an assignment to do something positive in that area tomorrow. Then, on a daily basis, check the list of suggestions and make it a task to accomplish one more objective each day.

Take a moment after each day and reflect on your efforts. What small thing did you learn in the process? In what ways could you be proud of yourself? Can you think of other ways unique to you that could help increase your communication range? If so, make it a specific assignment to learn about this during one of your next few days. Continue on your never-ending cycle of self-improvement with the conviction that multiple benefits will naturally come your way over time.

THE BOTTOM LINE

Remember that in order to "talk like a winner" in the broadest sense, you must "learn like a winner" as well. All you have to do is follow a a simple and powerful rule: *Stretch your communication range.* Once you appreciate the significance of this essential part of successful communication, it's only a matter of playing around with the ideas, adding your own creativity, practicing with greater intention, and testing it every day in your own life until it becomes a natural part of you. If you fall in love with the process, it's really that easy!

RIP

Three

Assess

DETERMINE THE TYPE OF SITUATION YOU'RE FACING

"Recognition of function always precedes recognition of being."

Rita Mae Brown
Author of *Starting from Scratch* (1988)

assess: 1. to determine the meaning, significance, or value of something. 2. to evaluate the pros and cons of a challenging situation in order to decide on an effective strategy for success. 3. as it applies to this book, the ability to observe and then determine the type of situation that you're about to face so that you can act in the most appropriate manner.

You're One More Step Closer To Unleashing The Winner Within! *People often jump into conversations with little regard for the context or circumstances of the situation. However, it's not normally appropriate to be the funny man or woman at a funeral. It's also not a great idea to be the most somber person at a 4th of July celebration. One of your main objectives as a master communicator will be to assess situations accurately before launching yourself into any conversation. That way, you'll converse in an appropriate manner no matter what the state of affairs is.*

Peyton Manning is the All-Pro quarterback of the Indianapolis Colts NFL (National Football League) football team. Manning set a record in 2006 for the most seasons with 4,000+ yards passing – an amazing seven. His success as a quarterback has earned him several awards including the NFL's Most Valuable Player, the NFL's Offensive Player of the Year, and the 2007 Super Bowl Most Valuable Player.

To watch Peyton Manning direct his team on a touchdown drive is a thing of beauty for football enthusiasts. More than any other NFL quarterback in recent history, Manning is particularly adept at assessing an opponent's defense and changing an offensive play at the last moment. Opposing defensive teams know that whatever they do to stifle the offense of the Indianapolis Colts will likely be met with smart split-second adjustments made by quarterback Peyton Manning.

Whether you're a quarterback playing in the National Football League or someone about to engage in a conversation with another person, it's important to assess a situation carefully before launching into your plan of action. When your assessments are accurate, the actions that you take will have a better chance of succeeding in any field of endeavor.

Casualness May Cause Casualties

Doing a poor job of assessing a situation can lead to some embarrassing behavior which people will *always* remember you for.

I recall the day when my brother, Glen, got married to Ellen. My family is of Japanese decent while Ellen's family is of Chinese decent. For those of you who are not very familiar with these cultures, I'll mention that there has always been a long-standing and sometimes bitter rivalry between our two ethnic groups. As a result of this rivalry, Glen's "China vs. Japan" wedding was especially significant to my older relatives. I remember my Aunt Elsie pulling me aside to make a point of telling me to behave myself so that I wouldn't embarrass our clan. Evidently, my reputation as a silly cut-up was not something that my Aunt Elsie wanted me to bring to this landmark social occasion.

After a traditional Chinese wedding, an informal reception was held in the afternoon primarily for the benefit of friends and business associates of Glen and Ellen. Later that evening, a more formal dinner party had been scheduled for close family members. As a member of the wedding party, I was chosen to sit at the head table with my brother's in-laws. Glen's in-laws and extended family are influential members of the Chinese-American community in the East Bay area of Northern California, so my brother was hoping (or more likely, praying) that I would make a good first impression at this formal dinner.

Unfortunately, I didn't assess the situation very well at the time and thought of the wedding reception as a fun time to drink a lot and party. When the first course of the reception dinner was being served, I started grabbing the food with my hands and eating. Glen shot me a quick look and said, "Steve, would you please wait for everyone else!" Not only was it rude of me to eat before anyone else, but according to Chinese tradition it's particularly disrespectful to the elders in a family. It didn't occur to me at the time that Glen was fearful that my embarrassing behavior might cause his influential in-laws to think that our family had no class or even further that Japanese-American people in general didn't have any class either.

While my display of poor manners and inebriated state might have earned me some polite laughter, I lost the all-important and more highly-valued respect of Glen's new in-laws. To this day, the relationship between the two families is only civil at best and my behavior at the wedding dinner party certainly didn't help matters. At least I didn't make matters worse at that dinner table by asking my brother's new father-in-law in my native Southern California surfer dialect, "Dude! How gnarly was that Peking Duck?"

The lesson here is to choose the proper social behavior for whatever occasion you find yourself in. That way, you'll build your key relationships correctly from the start with the ideal mix of admiration and respect. Sometimes, all the apologizing in the world can't make people forget about one poor assessment that results in inappropriate behavior for an important situation.

RULE #3: DETERMINE THE TYPE OF SITUATION YOU'RE FACING

Sizing up situations is something I'm sure you already do in certain cases. For instance, don't you sometimes assess an upcoming occasion, such as a friend's party, to determine what type of clothes to wear? Well, we should make a similar kind of evaluation in deciding what type of communication style to use, as well. By doing some smart research beforehand, you can avoid wearing the wrong outfit as well as communicating in an inappropriate and potentially embarrassing manner for an important occasion.

To help you gain more skill in assessing social situations, here are key questions to sharpen your awareness:

- **Who exactly are you dealing with?** Sometimes you will already be aware of someone's reputation or history, and this will give you clues for your interaction. Other times, you'll have to do some research in order to attain more precise background about who you're about to converse with. But in most situations, you will also have to seek first to understand how other people are feeling or thinking at a particular moment. Once you've gained a firm grasp of where others are coming from, you can adjust your conversation in a manner that is more suitable for the other people involved.

- **How many people will be participating?** The basic rule here is to allow about equal "talking time" for each individual in the conversation. So as a general guideline, if there are four people in the conversation, then each person should have ample opportunity to speak for about one-fourth of the time. When one person monopolizes a conversation, it's guaranteed to annoy the other people who don't get a fair chance to share. Just because other people in a group conversation don't speak up, doesn't mean that they want *you* to keep talking.

- **How much time do you have to talk?** Sometimes people will be in a hurry and have more pressing matters to handle. These people don't have a lot of time to spend talking with you. If you're unsure about this, ask them politely at the outset, *"Do you have a few moments?"* That question will give the other person a chance to answer truthfully and they're usually appreciative of this considerate action. Oftentimes, people will enter into a conversation out of politeness before they realize that it's going to take more time than they initially anticipated.

- **Where and when are you interacting?** There are certain places that are not conducive to talking for any length of time. Examples of this would be locations that are too cold, dark, noisy, crowded, busy, or uncomfortable in any way. In these environments, it's better to simply say "hello" and let the other person know that you'd love to talk to them under better circumstances. The same applies to the time of day. If the time is either very early or very late, you will probably want to check with the other person to see if it's okay to talk at length.

- **What activity will you be doing?** The activity that surrounds your conversation will often determine whether it will be a formal or informal occasion. Certain activities will lean more towards being informal, like those centered on recreation and leisure. But other activities that are related to work and career can be more formal in nature. The style you pick for dressing appropriately for an occasion is sometimes a good indicator of how you should approach your conversation as well.

- **How should you act in a semi-formal occasion?** Many people make embarrassing errors of judgment when the activity lies in the gray area between formal and informal. The key here is to separate the dominant behavior from the minor one. Let's say that you're attending a company Christmas party at a nice restaurant. This would be a more formal activity, but there are exceptions when the conversation can be more informal. The important point to remember is that inappropriate behavior at such an event may have negative ramifications towards your career. A classic example would be if you got too drunk at that Christmas party or ran your mouth with foul language in front of your boss. While this party may have been meant for you to have a good time, it didn't mean that anything goes like a wild night with your closest friends in Las Vegas.

☺ **How should you act in a semi-casual situation?** We have all been in this kind of environment, but have rarely tried to identify it. As a result, we can misjudge the situation and make costly communication and relationship mistakes. An example of this semi-casual situation is when you go to a fun or interesting activity with people who you don't know yet. A lot of people have their guard up initially and it's important that you establish rapport before acting silly, stupid, crazy, quirky, or outrageous. A little bit of formal politeness may earn you some points in the beginning of any new relationship as a sign of respect towards the other person. It's a much safer and wiser way to behave than assuming that anything goes in every situation that appears to be casual in nature.

By sizing up the situation accurately, you will avoid costly mistakes in your communication. That will help you establish a fine reputation for yourself as someone who acts appropriately regardless of the environment, activity, or situation.

REASSESS A PAST SITUATION NOW!

Think of a moment in the past when you were guilty of not sizing up the situation properly. Perhaps it was going to an after-hours gathering of co-workers, meeting new people through friends, or engaging in an activity that seemed somewhat foreign to you.

Now from the preceding discussion, pinpoint what caused your error in judgment. Did you overlook or make a wrong judgment about who you were dealing with? Did you fail to factor in how many people were participating, what time of day it was, where you were interacting, or how much time you had to talk? Or was it a simple matter of acting too casual for a formal event or being too formal for a casual event?

> "Every great mistake has a halfway moment, a split second when it can be recalled and perhaps remedied."
>
> Pearl S. Buck
> Nobel Prize-Winning Author (1892-1973)

The purpose of this exercise is to become more aware during the social situations you face in your life. If you factor in all the variables mentioned in this chapter, it will help you anticipate the proper way to converse so that you can be more effective in all of your relationships with others.

THE BOTTOM LINE

Remember that in order to "talk like a winner" in the broadest sense, you must "assess like a winner" as well. All you have to do is follow a simple and powerful rule: *Determine the type of situation you're facing.* Once you appreciate the significance of this essential part of successful communication, it's only a matter of playing around with the ideas, practicing with a definite intention, and putting it to the test regularly in your own life until it becomes a natural part of you.

Four

Smile

START YOUR CONVERSATIONS IN A FRIENDLY WAY

"Let us always meet each other with a smile, for the smile is the beginning of love."

Mother Teresa
Missionary & religious leader (1910-1997)

smile: 1. to display a facial expression that customarily indicates pleasure, friendliness, or amusement. 2. to express or appear to express approval or kindness. 3. as it applies to this book, the simplest and often most effective way to begin almost any face-to-face interaction with another person.

You're Another Step Closer To Unleashing The Winner Within! *Unfriendly habits make other people feel uneasy right from the start. Your job as a master communicator is to greet every person you meet in a friendly manner so that they can feel the natural warmth of your kindness, acceptance, and recognition. Except for the more serious circumstances, a warm and enthusiastic smile creates the best starting point for a mutually enjoyable conversation.*

When you walk into any Wal-Mart department store in the United States or Canada, you'll be greeted quickly in many cases by a smiling employee who hands you a shopping cart and says, "Hello, welcome to Wal-Mart." These "people greeters," as Wal-Mart calls them, take care of the store entrance appearance along with welcoming customers as they come in to shop.

Wal-Mart is a Fortune 500 company that has become known for its friendly "people greeters." As far back as 1968, Sam Walton, the founder of Wal-Mart, understood that people entering his stores are choosing to spend their hard-earned money with him. Walton wanted to show these customers how much he appreciated their business.

We could all learn a simple lesson for success that Wal-Mart has been demonstrating for many years: *Begin every interaction with a friendly greeting.* A smile and a sincere "hello" won't cost you any money, but their emotional effect on people is, without a doubt, *priceless.*

AWAKEN YOUR GENUINE SMILE FROM WITHIN

According to Dr. Martin Seligman, author of *Authentic Happiness,* there are two kinds of smiles, the "Duchenne smile" and the "Pan American smile." Dr. Seligman describes these two smiles in the following way:

> "The first smile called Duchenne smile (named after researcher Guillaume Duchenne) is genuine. The corners of the mouth turn up and the skin around the corners of your eyes crinkle. The other smile, called the Pan American smile (named after the flight attendants in television advertisements for the now-defunct airline), is inauthentic."

In our own lives, we've all tried to smile for a photograph by saying the word "cheese." But when we finally see that photograph, the smile may not look authentic because genuine emotion perhaps was not present. In other words, we offered a "Pan American" or "professional" smile to the camera lens.

TAKING A BUNCH OF LOUSY AUTHOR PHOTOS

A few months ago, I hired a professional photographer to take some new shots of me for my upcoming publicity campaign. I met the photographer at his studio for about an hour. After we finished with our photo session, he told me

avp

that he was going to touch up the final images before sending them back for approval.

When the photos finally arrived at my home a week later, I was really disappointed to find that there wasn't a single shot that I actually liked. All of the photos appeared to me to show the same thing – a forced smile with no genuine emotion. In the end, this particular photo session had turned out to be a complete waste of time and money.

On the recommendation of friend in the book industry, I hired another photographer named Dave who turned out to be a really fun and likeable guy. We took a bunch of new photos – some serious and others with me just clowning around. It turned out later that some of my best shots were the ones of me playing around for the fun of it.

An example of one of these better pictures appears on the opposite page. I'm holding a volleyball in the same pose that professional beach volleyball players take for some of their promotional photos. The smile on my face is real because I'm genuinely having a fun time posing like a pro when in fact I play the sport like a true amateur.

The point here is that you must possess inner feelings of warmth, excitement, and joy in order to radiate a genuine smile. When you have real positive emotion behind your smile, you can be more effective with other people than you would be by acting with only politeness or courtesy.

Remember, by beginning in a friendly manner with a true eagerness to share, you will be developing one of the smartest communication habits for establishing or building important personal and professional relationships.

RULE #4: START YOUR CONVERSATIONS IN A FRIENDLY WAY

As a rule of thumb, it's best to start off any interaction in a friendly way. True, there can be exceptions to this rule when the situation is serious, hostile, or grim. But, overall, strive to get rid of any unfriendly habits. This will help improve your interactions with others immensely.

Here are some important reminders of things to do in order to start your conversations in a friendlier manner:

- **Be the first one to offer a greeting**. Many people have a natural tendency to avoid making the first move when it comes to greeting someone. After all, you can avoid rejection and disapproval by simply choosing not to engage at all. But this behavior can be easily interpreted by other people to mean that you're acting unfriendly towards them. One of the simplest ways to develop more amiable habits is to be the first one to address people instead of waiting for them to reach out to you.
- **Begin with a friendly smile**. Take off on the right foot by starting your friendly interaction with a warm smile. This often causes the other person to smile in response. While smiling may not come naturally to you during the course of a difficult day, make sure that in the brief moment that you first engage someone that you at least suspend your negative thoughts. Then give the other person a smile of approval, which may also have the positive side-benefit of perking yourself up as well.
- **Remember to smile with your eyes**. If your smile looks phony to other people, they'll think that you don't mean it. When you greet others with a less than genuine smile, it

doesn't signal that you like or approve of them. Instead, it conveys that you're only acting polite or being courteous towards them. As mentioned earlier, a real smile includes the tightening of the muscles around the eyes while a fake one only involves the muscles around the mouth. If you want to smile like you mean it, make sure that your eyes are sending the same message as your mouth.

☺ **Develop a first-class greeting**. Do you ever notice how easily some people can come up to you, look you in the eyes, smile, shake your hand or give you a hug, and say, *"It's great to see you"*? I'm sure you can also recall other times when people have hardly acknowledged you and this made you wonder if these people don't like you for some unknown reason. If your goal is to get rid of your old unfriendly habits, then get comfortable with an assortment of greetings and friendly gestures that you can use at the start of every interaction. Watch others for ideas.

☺ **Talk in a friendly tone.** In addition to easily offering a greeting, warm smile and kind gestures, make sure that the words you choose are said in friendly tones. Researchers from the University of California at Los Angeles found that as much as 38% of communication is made by vocal tones alone! This means that if the tone of your voice is not friendly, the people you meet will not feel the full effect of your warmth and acceptance no matter what words you actually say.

☺ **Act like you're happy to see them.** When you're happy and excited to encounter another person, your natural warmth and enthusiasm come out easily. But there may be times when you might be preoccupied with other concerns and fail to show your delight about being in the presence of others. In this latter case, it would be easy to misinterpret your lack of warmth for being unfriendly rather than with being preoccupied with your own problems. The solution is to pay close attention to other people in the greeting process so that you can act warmly toward them. Do this instead of remaining in your own funk and causing people to wonder why you don't seem pleased about seeing them.

Remember to say their name. A simple technique that many people use in the business world is to remember to say a person's name several times during the course of a conversation. Dale Carnegie, author of *How To Win Friends And Influence People,* wrote, "Remember that a person's name is to that person the sweetest and most important sound in any language." The trick here is to avoid using this technique excessively or in an awkward manner where it appears too contrived. But if you can do this elegantly, it accomplishes two primary objectives: (1) it is appreciated by the other person, and (2) it helps you remember the other person's name for future references.

When you see the value in other people and can remain in a positive emotional state, it's easy to begin your conversations in a friendly manner. In addition, it's important to focus on breaking your unfriendly habits and establishing new ones like those above in order to make your greetings a well-received automatic habit.

Find One Unfriendly Habit To Stop Today!

One of the first tasks that you have to do is to identify your old unfriendly habits. Do you tend to avoid eye contact, walk around with a constant frown on your face, or wait for other people to say "hello" first? I'm sure that we've all done some of this from time to time, but the important thing here is to realize how these kinds of undesirable habits can ruin our own sense of joy and self-confidence.

For the next few days, try smiling at people who you don't know and even say "Hello!" on occasion. Notice how good you begin to feel inside about this new behavior and attitude toward others. Now pay attention when other people smile and look you in the eyes. Don't those simple acts of kindness and acceptance make you feel terrific as well?

People are very much the same. A simple act of friendliness causes people to naturally reciprocate in kind. And that sets off a pattern of behavior that's constructive to establishing healthy new relationships and improving the ones that you already have.

The Bottom Line

Remember that in order to "talk like a winner" in the broadest sense, you must "smile like a winner" as well. All you have to do is follow a simple and powerful rule: *Begin each conversation in a friendly way.* Once you understand the significance of this essential part of successful communication, it's only a matter of experimenting, practicing, and testing it every day in your own life until it becomes a part of you.

NEWS
MOVIE

Five

Choose

Select the Right Subjects to Discuss

"A gossip is one who talks to you about others; a bore is one who talks to you about himself; and a brilliant conversationalist is one who talks to you about yourself."

Lisa Kirk
American musical comedy actress

choose: 1. to select, pick out, or decide upon. 2. to judge the merits of multiple options in order to determine one course of action. 3. as it applies to this book, to determine which subjects are safe to discuss and which ones are to be wisely left alone.

You're One More Step Closer To Unleashing The Winner Within!
Some things are better left unsaid. One of your primary objectives as a master communicator is to steer away from unpleasant or unwanted topics that leave negative emotional residue on a conversation. That way, you'll have a greater chance of experiencing pleasurable conversations that encourage more frequent and enjoyable interactions in the future.

Jeopardy, known to many as America's favorite television quiz show, has an estimated 12 million viewers daily. The late media mogul Merv Griffin created the show's original concept back in 1964 in the dining room of his apartment in Beverly Hills, California. Since its 1984 syndicated debut, *Jeopardy* has been honored with over 25 daytime Emmy Awards to date and this is more than any other syndicated game show in television history.

Much of *Jeopardy's* success can be attributed to its unique answer-question format. Instead of our normal way of asking a question and receiving an answer, a contestant on the *Jeopardy* game show must think in reverse by receiving the answer first and then figuring out the original question. Far more than just a simple game of trivia, *Jeopardy* has become a stimulating test of knowledge that viewers find both entertaining and challenging.

For many people, conversations can also seem like games of trivia in which participants are going from topic to topic displaying their knowledge. But for more enlightened communicators, one-on-one conversations are about more than just showing off your intelligence. They're for bridging gaps between two people, sharing ideas and emotions, and exploring new avenues of expression. They are also sometimes about knowing what kinds of subjects to avoid discussing altogether.

How Will Your Audience Respond?

Do you want to engage in enjoyable conversations more often? Then it's important to know as much as you can about the people you're dealing with. This insight will provide safe terrain about which you can roam in light conversations. Then once you know more about where someone stands on certain sensitive issues, you can venture out more freely with topics to discuss. However, even then, there will be topics that you'll want to steer clear of as you speak with others.

When you bring up subjects that are uncomfortable, hurtful, or offensive to your listeners, they'll either get offended or lose interest in talking with you. In this regard, a good role model for what not to do is the character Larry David (who plays himself) on the hit HBO comedy series *Curb Your Enthusiasm.* During this popular half-hour program, we see Larry David at home and follow him on his adventures around town. Show after show, he appears clueless about how to navigate social situations without sticking his foot in his mouth and displeasing someone or ticking off a conversation partner. Some classic examples include Larry David's discussion of affirmative action upon meeting a high-powered black executive, his revelation when trying to change that the "Old Larry" hated his wife's sister, and his disclosure of which of their female friends he'd like to sleep with. Of course, because the show is a comedy, a conversational faux pas on Larry's part usually escalates in very funny ways.

Though the results of Larry David's communication missteps can be hilarious on the show, it wouldn't be much fun if you managed to annoy many of those around you with your comments and choice of subject matter. So in your own conversations, make sure that you consider your audience's probable reaction before taking a risk on more sensitive subjects. That way, you'll have people who want to stay around and participate more fully in your discussions.

RULE #5: SELECT THE RIGHT SUBJECTS TO DISCUSS

The topics that are talked about in a conversation will determine a lot about what emotions you and your listeners will experience. Therefore, there are subjects that you'd like to steer your focus toward and others that would be better off avoided.

The following guidelines are designed to keep your conversations on safe ground until you're more certain that everyone involved wants to explore other areas:

☺ **Don't start off by being too opinionated**. When first talking with people, invest some time easing into your conversations before expressing any strong opinions, beliefs, or convictions. This allows your listeners a chance to adjust to you and what you're about to discuss. Otherwise, you could blow people away with strong statements that they may not be prepared to hear and/or respond to comfortably. Making these kinds of comments should only be made in an appropriate situation and after you have fully qualified your remarks (saying, for instance *"Listen, I might be completely wrong on this one, but..."* or *"Please accept my apologies in advance if I'm out of line with this statement but..."*). If you express your ideas in this manner, you'll be unlikely to come across as being too opinionated or, even more annoying, self-righteous.

☺ **Be careful around sensitive issues.** We can do a lot of damage to key relationships by saying too much or revealing things that are better off being unsaid. That's not to say that you can't ever talk about important matters. I'm merely pointing out that in an initial social conversation, it's safer to avoid sensitive issues like politics, religion, money, and sex. Along the same vein, it's also wise to avoid prying into other people's business by asking questions that are too personal in nature. Once you've established a solid base of rapport, there will be more appropriate opportunities in the future when you can freely venture into these sensitive areas.

☺ **Focus on topics that interest others.** Your listeners will be more receptive to you when you talk in terms of their

"...but enough about me."

interests. *"What's in it for me?"* or *"What's significant about this?"* are questions that people naturally ask themselves unconsciously during many normal conversations. While you can't always find a topic that's of great interest to everyone involved in the conversation, it's certainly wise to avoid subjects that are of absolutely little or no value to anybody. By choosing topics that other people enjoy or find interesting, you'll have a better chance of getting a more lively exchange of ideas.

☺ **Know what you're talking about.** You don't want to waste other people's time by voicing strong or contradictory opinions on matters where you don't have any knowledge or personal experience. When your references are thin, be especially sure to mentally check your facts before speaking. Even then, it might be wise to admit what you *don't* know as well as what you *do* know about any given subject. This small act of honesty and humility will usually score some points for you. At the other extreme, make sure that you don't come across as a "know-it-all" by giving unsolicited advice. What you gain in respect for your display of knowledge may be lost in their affection towards you. But if people ask you first for your expertise, then by all means give them the best that you have to offer.

☺ **Take the more positive angle on a subject.** When in doubt, always choose the more upbeat side of a topic. That doesn't mean that you can't see both sides of an issue. What I'm saying is that by keeping the majority of the focus and time of a conversation on constructive, positive ideas, everyone will have a more overall enjoyable experience.

This usually rewards you with more enthusiastic, multi-person conversations than you would have if you talked too much or too long on negative, energy-draining subjects.

Stay informed about current events. If you want to relate to a wider range of people, be sure to stay current on the general topics of the day. You can keep abreast of things in our world by reading a quality newspaper, listening to talk radio shows, watching the national news on television, browsing the bookstore aisles, or skimming through magazines like *Newsweek, Time, Sports Illustrated, Business Week,* and *People.* You never know when a conversation will turn to a hot topic on business, lifestyle, politics, sports, national news, or international developments. You'll look a lot smarter in the eyes of others if you have something intelligent to say over a broad range of topics.

Don't spend major time on minor subjects. As a general rule, spend major time on major issues and only minor time on minor issues. A characteristic of low-achieving individuals is that they tend to spend the majority of their time talking about minor issues. A smart strategy is to assess the significance of a particular topic and give this topic its proper allotment of time. Then move on to other topics that have greater significance to your audience.

Part of being an excellent communicator is making sure that you select the right topics to talk about for a particular group of people. When you do this properly, it sets up your conversation so that it has a better chance of creating an enjoyable experience for everyone involved.

WHAT DO YOU TALK ABOUT REGULARLY?

During the next week, take a special note of the topics that you discuss with others in your daily conversations. Do you talk about the news of the day or more about the issues of your individual lives? Do your conversations contain an interesting mix of worthwhile or entertaining topics? Do you also prefer to talk exclusively about lightweight subjects?

Most importantly, are you satisfied with the choice of subjects that you regularly discuss with others? If your answer is "yes," then continue in that manner and expand your relationships with those who enrich your life with great content in your conversations. However, if you're not satisfied with your regular topics, review this chapter carefully. Come up with at least two or three ways to change your approach when it comes to selecting topics for discussion. In addition, make sure that you expand your social network so that you are around people who talk about things that matter more to you and relate to the brighter, more compelling future you envision for yourself.

THE BOTTOM LINE

Remember that in order to "talk like a winner" in the broadest sense, you must "choose like a winner" as well. All you have to do is follow a simple and powerful rule: *Select the right topics to discuss.* Once you appreciate the significance of this essential part of successful communication, it's only a matter of experimenting with the ideas, practicing with greater intention, and testing it regularly in your own life until it becomes a constructive new habit.

Six

Engage

GRAB THE ATTENTION OF YOUR LISTENERS

"He loved to talk better than hear and to dispute than to please. People generally left the room with a high opinion of that gentleman's parts and a confirmed resolution to avoid his society."

Hester Lynch Piozzi
English memoirist (1741-1821)

engage: 1. to obtain and hold someone's attention. 2. to involve oneself in a battle, conflict, or agreement. 3. as it applies to this book, the ability to enter into a conversation and gain the attention of others in a positive manner.

You're Another Step Closer To Unleashing The Winner Within! *People love to talk, but often hate to listen. When it's your turn to talk, make your points quickly and in an interesting manner so that your listeners aren't likely to get bored. Then step aside and allow your listeners a chance to do their share of the talking. If you do your part well, people will naturally be more eager to converse with you again in the future.*

If you don't have a mobile or cellular (cell) phone by now, then you're regarded by most people as living in the Stone Age. Everywhere you look, whether while you're driving around in your car, shopping in the grocery store, or waiting in line for coffee at Starbucks, you'll see people talking away on one of these modern communication devices.

Evidently, people who talk a lot on their phones are on a different calling plan than me. My calling plan includes 450 minutes a month at a cost of about $40. But if I go over my allotted minutes per month, I get penalized for additional time on the phone at 45 cents per minute. During one of my busiest months, I went over my phone minute limit and had to pay an additional $75 fee. Ever since then, I've been careful to avoid wasting time talking away on my cell phone with pointless chatter.

Whether you're talking on your cell phone with a limited calling plan or engaging in a face-to-face conversation with a close friend, be sure that you make good use of your time by having something of value to say and getting to your point quickly. In doing so, you'll help keep your listeners interested and eager for another lively conversation with you in the future. Don't make the common mistake of thinking that just because *you* want to talk, other people will be thrilled about listening for very long.

PEOPLE HAVE SHORT ATTENTION SPANS

Sometimes we forget just how short some people's attention spans can be at any given time. Take, for example, a situation we've all been in where you're sitting in your car stopped at a red traffic light. You might find yourself looking out the side window doing a little bit of daydreaming when the signal suddenly turns green. No more than a second later, you're almost guaranteed to hear the driver in the car behind you blasting their horn. It might have been only a second or two of waiting, but it's a reminder to you that some people can be very impatient.

A similar kind of impatience occurs often in our daily conversations. If we take too long in telling a personal story, people start getting annoyed at having to listen. Out of politeness, they may not interrupt us while we're speaking. But if there was a courteous way of honking their proverbial horns, they would certainly be on it quickly in order to get us to move along in our speaking!

Have you ever heard a professional stand-up comedian who is slow at getting to their points? The answer, of course,

"It is not hard to converse for a short space of time on subjects about which one knows little, and it is indeed often amusing to see how cunningly one can steer the conversational barque, hoisting and lowering her sails, tacking this way and that to avoid reefs, and finally racing feverishly for home with the outboard engine making a loud and cheerful noise."

Virginia Graham
Author of *Say Please* (1949)

* **barque:** a small sailing ship with three to five masts

is "no." That's because a comedian understands that the mind moves infinitely quicker than the spoken word. In order for the comedian to be effective, they must grab the attention of the audience with an interesting story or comment and move quickly to the punch line. A comedian who communicates slowly will bore their audiences and find themselves looking for a new line of work.

Whether you're a stand-up comic or a regular person wanting to communicate more effectively, it's important to talk in a manner that quickly appeals to your audience. That usually means that the time you spend talking should be short and sweet initially. It's only after each person has had a chance to speak that you can safely elaborate more fully on your end of the conversation.

RULE #6: GRAB THE ATTENTION OF YOUR LISTENERS

Once you realize that most people have a fickle attention span, it becomes your first priority to grab a secure hold of it as quickly as you can. Otherwise, you may go on and on about a topic without anyone else actually listening to you!

The following suggestions are designed to help you grab an audience's attention during the critical early moments of your conversation. If you get good at this, people will eagerly anticipate a lively conversation with you in the future.

- **Start off at a snappy pace.** Begin by speaking in short, simple sentences as a way of warming up. Sometimes this means being as basic as saying, *"Hi! How are you? What's up?"* Like Olympic sprinters in the 100 meter run, a lively two-way conversation may take a series of quick small steps before you can hit your stride. Do this instead of beginning a conversation with a long, uninterrupted monologue on your part. We've all endured that unpleasant experience at times from others.

Make a bold statement. Like the headlines on the front page of *The New York Times*, it takes a bold statement to grab someone's immediate attention. For example, around Valentine's Day, you can start off a conversation by saying, *"Flowers are a rip-off! The florist down the street is selling a dozen red roses for $100 plus $20 for delivery!"* Another example might be: *"Talk about terrible role models! The antics of Britney Spears and Lindsay Lohan are setting a terrible example for impressionable young women."*

Tease them with a question. If you've ever listened closely to a professional speaker, you'll notice that they often initiate their talks by asking their audiences a question. In fact, these speakers will frequently begin with the statement, *"Let me ask you a question."* Then they'll follow by asking something like: *"Has there ever been a time when you felt totally helpless or afraid?"* or *"Have you ever been in a situation where everyone knew each other and you were the lone stranger?"* By asking a leading question, the listener is forced to think. If done properly, this is an effective way to grab attention and involve your listeners quickly in a conversation with you.

Entice your audience with an inside secret. What better way is there to stir up your listener's curiosity, then to disclose an inside secret or reveal privileged information? The next time that you stand in line at the grocery store, take a moment to scan the magazines and notice how they entice potential buyers with catchy headlines like "Criminal Minds: Behind the Scenes (*TV Guide*)," "Secrets to More Energy (*Ladies' Home Journal*)," and "Where will you meet your next boyfriend? (*Cosmopolitan Magazine*)." When you know something interesting or important that someone else doesn't, it creates a natural response to pay attention to what you have to say.

☺ **Relay the hottest news.** With the growth of the Internet, news travels now at lightning speeds. But not everyone has the time or inclination to follow the news as it is developing. Examples of breaking news would include court verdicts (like the O.J. Simpson murder trial or Anna Nicole Smith estate ruling), celebrity mishaps (Britney Spears, Mel Gibson, Paris Hilton), sporting event outcomes (Who won the football game or boxing match?), and television show recaps (*American Idol* eliminations, *Survivor* finalists, or what happened the other night on *Grey's Anatomy?*). While hardly anyone cares to know the details of everything that is happening in the world, most people would be curious to know the highlights or headlines on the few subjects that are of particular interest to them.

☺ **Make people laugh or smile.** If you can get your audience to actually do something in the first 10 seconds, you'll greatly increase your chances of securing their attention. One of the best ways to do this is by using humor to prompt your listeners to laugh, chuckle, or smile. Excellent examples of folks who have this down pat are late night television talk show hosts like David Letterman, Jay Leno, and Jimmy Kimmel. If you closely watch these entertainers perform, you'll notice that an attempt at humor will come almost every minute!

- **Be excited about your subject.** If you're not enthusiastic about your subject, then your audience isn't going to feel that way either. Be sure that your topic is something that stimulates you and makes you eager to share it. That kind of emotion will naturally transfer to your listeners. If you can't find a convenient subject to be excited about, then shift your attention to playing the role of an attentive listener instead.

Getting off to a good start in a conversation requires you to engage quickly and effectively. Don't make the common mistake of assuming that people will naturally want to hear what you have to say. In today's busy world, a person may only be willing to hear the first sentence or two of what you want to share before deciding whether or not they're actually going to listen to you any longer.

WHAT NEW APPROACH WILL YOU TRY NEXT?

On a notepad (or in a personal journal if you have one), take a few moments now to list the common ways that you habitually begin your conversations. For example, I have a habit of starting off my conversations at a snappy pace. That's worked well for me in most cases. Still, I'm sure there are people who think that I'm too perky at times when they feel this doesn't seem to fit the occasion.

After you've completed this simple task, take a look at the list of suggestions in the previous section of this chapter. Find some approaches that you don't normally use and try them in your next conversations. Experiment with these new ways of engaging your audience and see if you are able to grab the attention of your listeners right from the start. This might feel a bit awkward at first, but realize that you need to develop more variety in how you start conversations. That way, you'll have the element of surprise working for you whenever someone chooses to enter into a conversation with you.

> **"Her conversation was like a very light champagne, sparkling but not mounting to the brain."**
>
> Gertrude Atherton
> Author of *Transplanted* (1919)

For many people, getting started in a conversation is the most challenging part. When you have a variety of interesting ways to engage yourself in a discussion, it will become easier for you to get your interactions off to a flying start.

The Bottom Line

Remember that in order to "talk like a winner" in the broadest sense, you must "engage like a winner" as well. All you have to do is follow a simple and powerful rule: *Grab the attention of your listeners.* Once you know and understand the significance of this essential part of successful communication, it's only a matter of playing around with the ideas, adding your own creativity, practicing with greater intention, and putting it to the test on a regular basis in your own life until it becomes a natural part of you. If you should ever feel discouraged on your journey to communication success, remind yourself that the natural ability to succeed already resides within you. You only have to uncover it!

THIS GUY
IS REALLY
GOOD!!

Seven

Express

Learn how to say it well

"There are very few people who don't become more interesting when they stop talking."

Mary Lowry
Author of *The Pacific Sun* (1985)

express: 1. to make it known with words. 2. to communicate your feelings, ideas, and opinions with others. 3. as it applies to this book, the ability to communicate in a way that clearly conveys the intention of your message while at the same time making it as enjoyable as possible for the listener.

You're Another Step Closer To Unleashing The Winner Within! *Many people believe that you're either born with the gift of gab or arrive into this world without it. In reality, brilliant conversationalists have developed and refined the skills of expression over the course of their entire lives. As a master communicator, you must consciously learn how to express yourself more effectively through serious study and practice with the purpose of getting better. That way, you'll acquire the skill and self-confidence that will enable you to have more influence in your key relationships.*

The Art Institute of Chicago, one of America's finest museums, has on display a painting by 19th century French artist, Georges Seurat, titled *A Sunday On La Grande Jatte* – 1884. The image, featuring a crowd of people visiting an island park on the Seine River just outside of Paris, is a favorite among the museum's visitors, and it is known around the world. What makes this piece of art so fascinating is Seurat's use of tiny, dot-like brush strokes of different colors which when viewed at a distance blend together beautifully. That Seurat was able to create such a brilliant and complex painting with the use of simple colored dots is truly an amazing display of artistry.

In a similar way, there are true masters at crafting the spoken language. And like with this famous piece of art by Georges Seurat, the creation of brilliant and complex verbiage can be accomplished with simple basic tools. For those aspiring to be more effective communicators, the idea is not to try to impress people overtly with your mastery of the language, but instead to express yourself brilliantly with simple use of "color," design, and clarity.

Sloppy Speaking May Lead To Your Downfall

The manner in which you express yourself with words is largely the same whether it's a conversation in private or a brief talk to a small group. The only real difference is that your effectiveness or lack thereof will increase as the numbers in your audience grow.

While in college at San Diego State University, I was nominated to run for the position of social chairman of my all-men's dormitory. At the time, I was a fun-loving freshman more interested in meeting coeds than I was in going to classes. My opponent in this election for social chairman of the dorm was a guy named Bill who ran the campus radio station and was a senior majoring in telecommunications.

For our election, the entire group of guys from the dorm crowded into a meeting room where each candidate was allowed five minutes to discuss his plans for the coming semester's social calendar. Bill went first and presented an articulate and entertaining talk for a full five minutes detailing his plans for our dorm. He mentioned hiking trips, concerts, volunteer work, beach outings, and study parties that involved women in the surrounding dormitories.

Then it came my turn to dazzle the crowd. Unfortunately, I wanted to run and hide instead of talk to this group of guys. After all, it really wasn't my idea to run for this position. A friend in the dorm nominated me basically because I was a friendly party-animal. With no experience speaking and a total lack of enthusiasm, I said to the crowd, "Basically, I'd like to find more ways where we can party with the chicks in the girls' dorms. That's really what we all want, isn't it? Uhh....I guess that's about it."

After my 20-second speech, Bill and I left the meeting for a few minutes so that the guys in the dorm could vote. When we walked back into the room, my opponent and I found everyone laughing. Apparently, they got a big kick out of me losing the election by a final vote of 84 to 1. My lone vote came from the friend who had nominated me. Not even a solitary other guy in the dorm voted for me. A buddy came up to me afterwards and said, "That was one of the funniest performances I've ever seen. You made a complete fool of yourself. It was absolutely hilarious!"

Fast-forward many years to the present and now I find myself giving speeches to groups concerning my books as well as serving as a seasonal professional tour guide. In both of my speaking roles, I have to be able to talk effectively on many diverse topics with clarity, humor, and good taste.

When I look back to that bumbling speech and compare it to my smooth radio interviews today, the difference amazes me. I attribute my progress over the years to my willingness to stretch my abilities and a lot of practice in doing something that I recognized as being significant to the quality of my life. Even the challenging tasks of becoming a skilled conversationalist or polished speaker are things that you can achieve when you make the commitment.

RULE #7: LEARN HOW TO SAY IT WELL

Most people make the mistake of thinking that speaking well has to do with using sophisticated words and poetic language, but this is rarely the case. What you really desire as a communicator is for other people to be affected in the way that you want.

The following guidelines will assist you in accomplishing this objective in your everyday conversations:

- **Focus more on expressing, less on impressing.** When someone tries too hard to impress others with what they know, it usually has a counterproductive effect. Most people also don't like someone who comes across as being Mr. or Ms. Know-It-All. It's a wiser strategy to concentrate on expressing your ideas enthusiastically on subjects that you know first-hand and feel eager to share. People will be more naturally impressed with your love for a relevant subject than with the actual content of your message.
- **Get to the point quickly**. After your greeting, transition into your topic with a summary line, or punch line, that links with the other person's agenda. For example, *"Here are three ways we could make our weekend nights out more fun."* Then organize your thoughts with just the necessary facts so that you move along in a logical fashion toward your final conclusion (as in the closing, *"If we do these three things, we can't help but have a great time when we go out"*). People will naturally tire of a speaker who rambles on without any

direction or purpose to their talk. The listener may come to the conclusion that the only reason this person wants to chat is to hear the sound of their own voice filling the air.

- **Resist the unwise urge to lie or exaggerate**. A good rule to follow is this: *Deal only in truths.* If the truth isn't good enough, then you're better off not saying anything at all. What people commonly do – in order to make up for what they don't know, what they've forgotten, or what may be dull in truth – is to lie or exaggerate. While it might be convenient to fudge on the truth in order to achieve a short-term outcome, the downside is that you could develop a reputation for being a liar or someone who can't be trusted for accuracy. Whether you're speaking or writing, the best policy is to check your facts thoroughly and state the truth so that others will trust the validity of your words with more confidence.

- **Clean up your language.** You'll never know the people who avoid you simply because the language that you use offends them. I'm not talking about being a "goodie goodie" and being afraid of expressing yourself freely. It's more about making sure that you don't lose unnecessary social opportunities because of distasteful word choices. Here are a few examples of common bad language choices and their corresponding alternative phrasings:

Kiss my ash!	My answer is no.
I don't give a fudge!	It's not a big concern of mine.
You've got to be sheeting me!	You're only kidding, right?
She's acting like a real beach!	Mary can be very assertive.
You can go rot in Helen!	People get what they deserve.

☺ **Develop a tasteful brand of humor.** If your sense of humor is characterized by others as being rude, crude, offensive, tasteless, gross, sick, dirty, morbid, or bizarre, then you should seriously consider making a change in this area. What you may gain with a short-term laugh might not be worth what you lose in long-term quality relationships. Sometimes people will try so hard to be funny in order to fill their emotional needs for being liked or accepted that they overlook how much it might cost them in terms of respect. But what's worse for the guilty offender is that they rarely see anything wrong with tasteless humor and never realize how it shrinks the size of their audience or limits their opportunities to associate with a better quality crowd.

☺ **Qualify your strong statements.** You can state your mind about almost anything amongst your closest friends. But around people who hardly know you, expect immediate resistance if you take strong positions on controversial topics. You can lower this resistance towards you by prefacing your remarks with comments like *"Please correct me if I'm wrong on this,"* or *"Based on my limited resources, I've gathered that..."* As I've mentioned, another smart thing to do is admit to your listeners what it is that you *don't* know about a particular topic. You can also be more on target if you ask for additional information about the nature of the topic under discussion before stating your opinions. That way, you'll avoid misjudging the significance of a conversation and overstating your position, when what's actually taking place is just a light exchange of ideas.

- **Be logical in your approach to content**. We know that in many cases a listener has only a short amount of time to hear what we have to say. Unless the matter is extremely sensitive, a great solution for this as the speaker is to present the most important piece of information in the narrative at the outset. Then you can fill in your conversation with items in diminishing importance. This allows the listener a chance to get the essential point you have to make without going through a long waiting period in order to understand where your conversation is going. In addition, keep your facts and reasoning to a minimum. It's easy to overwhelm people with too much information, especially if the conversation is more casual in nature.
- **Adjust your voice controls for easy listening.** Sometimes it's not what you say that matters as much as how you say it. Make sure that your voice qualities are pleasing to the ears. Adjust your volume so that you're not too loud to the point of being annoying or too soft where it's a strain to hear you. Check to see that you're enunciating clearly and vary the pitch and pace of your speaking voice so that you don't become monotone. The optimal strategy here is to become more aware of your voice qualities or patterns and then work on improving them constantly for the sake of your audiences.

When you express yourself in more effective ways, you'll build a reputation as someone who deserves listening ears. A better reputation allows you to say less because your words will have more weight than before. This will naturally create more balance between the time you spend talking and the time you spend listening.

LEARN JUST ONE NEW WORD A DAY!

Try filling out a crossword puzzle or playing a game of *Scrabble* and it may remind you just how limited your own vocabulary is right now. Whether or not you feel that way, you're likely to benefit from expanding your vocabulary. Having more words at your disposal can improve your ability to be more personally expressive.

During the next week, begin a new habit of consciously increasing your vocabulary by learning at least one new word a day. A convenient way to do this task is to buy a "Word-of-the-Day" calendar at your local bookstore. You can also read newspapers, magazines, books, or online articles in your search for any words that you don't understand. (When you come across a word that you're unclear about, jot it down on a piece of paper and look the word up in a dictionary for a list of definitions and proper uses.) Once you've selected a word through either method, make the commitment to use that word a few times during the day. That way, you'll be building a better vocabulary one small step at a time. After the first week, consider continuing this process of acquiring new words as a helpful or entertaining process.

THE BOTTOM LINE

Remember that in order to "talk like a winner" in the broadest sense, you must "express like a winner" as well. All you have to do is follow a simple and powerful rule: *Learn how to say it well.* Once you appreciate the significance of this essential part of successful communication, it's only a matter of practicing with a sense of purpose and testing it every day in your own life until it becomes a natural part of you.

TOO COCKY.

Eight

Impact

Say it with the proper emotion

"Human relations are built on feeling, not on reason or knowledge. And feeling is not an exact science; like all spiritual qualities, it has the vagueness of greatness about it."

Amelia E. Barr
Author of *The Belle of Bowling Green* (1904)

impact: 1. to create a significant emotional effect on another human being. 2. to have a memorable or persuasive influence on others by the manner in which you communicate. 3. as it applies to this book, the ability to express yourself in a way that leaves a deep, desirable impression on another person.

You're One More Step Closer To Unleashing The Winner Within!
Most people believe that it's only the words you select that create your communication with others. But studies have shown that the way we use our physical bodies (facial expressions, eye contact, hand gestures, etc.) and the tone of our voices sends a stronger message to our audiences than do the actual words we present. One of your primary objectives as a master communicator is to realize that the reasoning of your words is not as powerful as the emotions that you convey with your non-verbal language. That way, you can have a bigger impact and a greater influence on the people in your life, now and in the future.

Eldrick "Tiger" Woods is widely regarded as the greatest professional golfer of our time. At age 32, he has won more major championships and had more wins on the Professional Golf Association Tour than any other active golfer. Tiger's achievements on the golf course have also made him one of the highest paid professional athletes in the world for the last several years.

Golf in its simplest terms is a sport where an individual hits a ball into a hole using a variety of clubs. A top pro like Tiger

Woods is a master at selecting the appropriate club for hitting the golf ball with the right amount of distance, trajectory, and accuracy.

Likewise, a master communicator must be able to select the right words for the right occasion and deliver their message to listeners with the desired degree of emotion. That way, a person can connect naturally with other people on the appropriate emotional level where their impact and influence will be felt most.

Beware Of Too Much Or Too Little Firepower!

When referring to using well-measured emotion for the appropriate occasion, business philosopher E. James Rohn advised, "In leadership, we teach you not to shoot a cannon at a rabbit. It's too much fire power. It's effective, but you'll have no more rabbit."

Many people make this common mistake in their communication when they confront a friend or business associate by asking them bluntly, "What's wrong with you?" They choose these words instead of using the softer and more elegant question, "What seems to be troubling you?" The first comment sounds more like a personal attack, while the second statement comes across as more of a compassionate inquiry.

While appearing on *The Oprah Winfrey Show* in May 2005, actor Tom Cruise displayed love for his then-fiancé Katie Holmes with a classic example of too much emotional fire power. When questioned about the nature of his romance, Cruise started jumping euphorically on Oprah's couch and punching the air while yelling about his love for Katie. This crazy behavior earned Cruise the #1 ranking on the *TV Guide* poll of "Wildest Celebrity Meltdowns," topping such memorable moments as Michael Jackson dangling his baby from a hotel balcony in Berlin and Farrah Fawcett acting disoriented on the *Late Show with David Letterman.* Going over-the-top with too much emotion usually communicates a negative message instead of a positive one. Tom Cruise's bizarre behavior on *The Oprah Winfrey Show* didn't convince the public about his love for Katie Holmes so much as it created serious doubts about his sanity and/or sensibility.

> **"Spilling your guts is just exactly as charming as it sounds."**
>
> Fran Lebowitz
> Author of *Social Studies* (1977)

As an aspiring master communicator, you want to be mindful of avoiding major expressions of emotions for minor occasions (which, when used, can blow people away with too much firepower). At the same time, you also don't want to miss an opportunity to affect others by only using minor emotions on things that do have major significance. The secret to successful communication is to size up the situation accurately and choose the right amount of the appropriate emotions for the occasion that you face.

RULE #8: SAY IT WITH THE PROPER EMOTION

We all have our own natural tendencies for how we express ourselves emotionally. There are areas or situations where we might tend to be either too weak or too strong in our communication with others. As a result, we may not have the impact on people that we desire.

The following ideas are designed to keep your communication more on target so that you can affect others with your intended impact:

- **Be humorous without being silly.** In the attempt to lighten the mood or to get people to like us, we often inject humor into our conversations. The catch here is to make sure this humor is tasteful and appropriate. When you overdo it with humor, you risk being perceived as someone who is silly. For instance, I have a friend who likes to make funny faces while in public, which is fine with little children. But when my friend does this around people his own age, he comes across as foolish. When you play the humor card too frequently, others might regard you as stupid, weak-minded, or silly instead of your original aim of being fun, light-hearted, and entertaining.
- **Be serious without being grim.** On issues that matter, we all would like to be taken seriously. But at the same time, we don't want to be labeled as merely a serious person. The part of being serious that's attractive is possessing the wisdom to separate what's significant from what's trivial. For example, it would be wise to be serious about hiring an excellent doctor for a surgery or a skilled lawyer to represent you in a lawsuit. But on a more social or everyday level, we usually don't need that same degree of seriousness. When you carry yourself too much of the time in a

serious manner, people can't help but think of you as being grim, negative, and simply no fun to be around. If you tend to be more on the serious side, make sure to mix in some lighter conversations so that others will feel comfortable with you.

Be playful without being obnoxious. Being a person who is free-spirited and full of fun is often labeled as being "playful." But when someone overdoes it with their playfulness, they start becoming obnoxious or annoying to others. For example, I've always gotten a big rise out of teasing and making fun of my friends. It has been done with a smile and usually is meant in jest. But from time to time, I've gotten bad reactions from others when I've unwisely chosen the wrong time and place to poke fun at them. Rather than regarding me as being "playful," my victims have often thought I was acting more like an obnoxious creep.

Be lively without being antsy. Being full of life, energetic, and passionate are highly-valued qualities that we all want to possess within ourselves on a daily basis. Lacking these qualities makes us appear dull, if in fact we are even noticed at all. On the other hand, we can go too far in our quest to appear lively by coming across as being hyperactive, nervous, or keyed up. These undesirable qualities cause others to feel uncomfortable when they are in our company for any extended period of time.

Be colorful without being weird. Going to an author/speaker seminar is always an interesting event for me because of the diverse group of people that I meet there. While writers have been traditionally known as being introverts, the new breed coming into this industry is composed of more passionate, colorful, and somewhat outrageous personalities. While being colorful is almost a "must" for self-promotion, going too far and being strange or weird is a turn-off in any field. Be careful in your attempt at self-expression and gaining attention that you measure your stride and stay within the range of appropriate behavior.

Be confident without being cocky. Being arrogant or cocky is often confused with genuine self-confidence. The major difference is that cocky people gain their sense of power by putting other people down. On the other hand, a truly confident person is skilled at building themselves up from within, knowing that you also strengthen yourself as a natural by-product of improving the self-worth of others. On the surface, being confident and being cocky can appear to be the same. But the difference may be felt in the person's intention as well as the residual feeling, good or bad, that is left long after a conversation has occurred.

Be classy without being condescending. It's a well-accepted compliment to be regarded as refined, stylish, sophisticated, and elegant. These elements of class will help distinguish you from others whenever people make comparisons for any reason. The key here is for you to avoid putting down those who aren't up to speed or as good as you are in any particular area. The act of patronizing others or feeling that you're superior to them will be easily noticed in your voice tones and facial expressions.

It's a truly classy individual who presents themselves at their best, but at the same time possesses the warmth, kindness, and compassion to bond through the heart with other people regardless of who they might be.

☺ **Be casual without being sloppy.** How we dress and present ourselves is often a mirror image of our preferred style of conversation. In both cases, while it's fine to be casual, it's rarely attractive or desirable to come across as being sloppy or careless. Like a drunk person in a bar, a sloppy conversationalist will not be discreet about what topics to bring up, what emotions to express, and how to react to what others say. Just remember to avoid being too careless in your conversations or else other people won't take you seriously when it matters most.

By following these guidelines, you can keep your emotions in check so that you don't scare people away by being too over-the-top or lull people to sleep by flying too low under the radar. Sometimes these simple distinctions can mean a world of difference to those who aspire to build solid long-term relationships with a wide range of people.

WHERE ARE YOUR COMMUNICATION BLIND SPOTS?

From the preceding list of topics, find one or two desirable items that you often see missing in friends, family members, neighbors, co-workers, or business associates. Do you think that these people are aware of the fine line between how they communicate and how you perceive them?

Now it's your turn to access yourself. From this same list, find one idea for you to work on in the next day or week.

Take the time now to write down your intention. (Example: Just for today, I will be casual without being sloppy or just for today, I will be colorful without being weird.) Continue through this list until you've had a chance to work on all eight refinements of emotional communication.

"The knowledge of ourselves is a difficult study, and we must be willing to borrow the eyes of our enemies to assist the investigation."

Hannah Farnham Lee
Author of *The Log-Cabin* (1844)

Like the people you've identified two paragraphs earlier, we are not aware of our own blind spots when it comes to how we affect other people with our communication habits. Since honest, accurate feedback is rare and difficult to find, an aspiring master communicator like yourself must resort to working from a detailed checklist, such as the pointers in this chapter, in order to impact people in the way you desire.

The Bottom Line

Remember that in order to "talk like a winner" in the broadest sense, you must "impact like a winner" as well. All you have to do is follow a simple and powerful rule: *Say it with the proper emotion.* Once you know and understand the significance of this essential part of successful communication, it's only a matter of playing around with the ideas, adding your own creativity, practicing with a greater sense of purpose, and testing it regularly in your own life until it becomes a constructive new habit. If this seems really easy to you, that's because the ability of succeed already resides inside of you. The only thing you have to do is rediscover it.

Nine

Re-live

TELL INTERESTING PERSONAL STORIES

"Storytelling reveals meaning without committing the error of defining it."

Hannah Arendt
Author of *Men in the Dark Times* (1968)

relive: 1. to experience something again. 2. to use the imagination to recreate a memorable experience. 3. as it applies to this book, the ability to recapture the original energy, color, and emotion of a personal experience with the magic of your own communication mastery.

You're Another Step Closer To Unleashing The Winner Within! *You can inadvertently bore people to death by telling long, uninterrupted personal stories that offer no entertainment value whatsoever. At the same time, people may take you too lightly if you don't have much to say in conversations either. One of your main objectives as a master communicator is to learn how to effectively tell an interesting personal story with the freshness and color that grabs and holds an audience's attention. That way, you can naturally affect other people emotionally with each tale you share.*

On Christmas morning 2006, one of the gifts that I opened was an audio CD titled *Love* by the Beatles. This music is a collection of experimental mixes using original Beatles master tapes, and it was designed as a soundtrack for a Cirque Du Soleil show of the same name that plays at the Mirage Hotel in Las Vegas.

Famed music producer Sir George Martin and his son Giles developed this interesting mix of vintage Beatles music and in doing so created the first new Beatles material in 10 years. Speaking of the *Love* project, Giles Martin said, "What people will be hearing on the album is a new experience, a way of re-living the whole Beatles musical lifespan in a very condensed period."

Upon its release, the new *Love* album immediately became the top-selling music CD in America. At the same time, the new Cirque Du Soleil *Love* production is being touted as one of the hottest show tickets in Las Vegas today.

Whether it's the new Beatles "Love" material or a personal story that you get to tell, people will enjoy a new experience when you re-live the past in a fresh way. With that approach, people will eagerly look forward to being entertained by the way you speak in future conversations.

THE OLDER WE GET, THE BETTER WE WERE

Every other year, a group of my friends from junior high and high school get together with our wives and girlfriends in San Diego for an informal reunion. My friend Charlie Somol hosts this fun event at the restaurant he owns called *Good Time Charlie's Bar & Grill.* Most of the guys in this group shared a lot of experiences together including playing Little League baseball, learning how to surf, dating the same group of girls, and going through the typical adolescent struggles that defined growing up in our era.

In the first hour of the reunion at *Good Time Charlie's*, we go through the regular formalities of updating others on how we're each doing in our present lives. The conversations usually cover topics about our families, old friends, career changes, travel adventures, and health concerns. We behave like responsible mature adults until the effects of alcohol start kicking in and then the party really takes off.

At these gatherings, I always run into my old Little League baseball teammate Matt Victor. Matt and I have a ritual whereupon first seeing him at an event, I immediately go into the following animated replay of our life's biggest moment together as 12-year-old boys:

"There's one out in the last inning of the Silver Spur Little League Baseball Championship game and our team is leading by only one run. The batter hits a sharp ground ball to Matt at third base. He fields the ball and shoots it over to me at first base for the second out. As this is happening, the runner that was on second base heads to third base. I quickly throw the baseball back to Matt at third base, but the ball is low and bounces away from him. Instinctively, the runner on third base heads towards home with a chance of tying up the ballgame. But Matt recovers the ball quickly and fires a perfect throw to home plate. Our pitcher happens to be standing out-of-position a few feet down the third base line in front of home plate. He intercepts Matt's throw to the catcher and tags the runner out on the top of head just before he has a chance to score. We suddenly realize this is the third out and the end of the game. All of us kids break out into a wild celebration on the field. And that's how Matt and I became the Silver Spur Little League Baseball Champions!"

Matt and I light up with excitement each time our baseball story gets retold. Matt's wife smiles, rolls back her eyes, and shakes her head as she reminds us, "That story seems to get better every year." Matt and I then laugh together with the realization that this one story creates a special bond that he and I will always share for the rest of our lives.

Whether it's re-living a treasured memory from childhood or sharing a seemingly small incident that happened in your everyday life, it's the interesting way that you retell your personal stories that will naturally impact other people. When other folks are able to re-live and enjoy the spirit of your experiences, they'll have a natural tendency to connect with you emotionally.

RULE #9: TELL INTERESTING PERSONAL STORIES

Many people mistakenly believe that good storytelling is a God-given ability. But on closer examination, you'll discover that good storytellers have mastered their craft from a combination of good role models, conscious efforts, and years of everyday practice.

To help you improve more rapidly in this overlooked and underappreciated area, here are some key points to consider carefully:

- **Say up front that it's going to be quick.** Before you begin launching into your story, let your audience know that you're going to be brief. Right at the beginning say, *"I've got a quick story for you"* or *"This will only take a minute."* This alerts your listeners to pay attention for only a short period of time, which is something that most people are willing to do. After you've done this, it's up to you to deliver on your promise by making your story brief, briskly paced, and to the point.
- **Don't waste time setting the scene.** Cut to the chase and spend as little time as possible describing the circumstances of your story. If your audience is captivated by your

narrative, they'll naturally ask you for more details after you finish. Your objective in sharing an anecdote is to give your audience a taste of your experience. Give them the short version and then if there's more time and sufficient interest, you can fill in the details later.

㉿ **Re-live an action moment immediately.** Within the first 10 seconds, make a point of getting right into the action. An example of this would be to say, *"Last Tuesday afternoon, I was walking across the street and out of the corner of my eye I saw a huge truck coming straight for me. I was thinking to myself, 'I'd better jump out of the way or else I'm a goner.'"* The key here is to secure your audience's attention while you have it. The first 10 seconds are critical. If you don't start off well, then you risk losing your audience's interest for the remainder of your story.

㉿ **Replay the exact dialogue.** Like a tape recorder, rewind any interesting sound bites that you have in your story and replay them for your audience. Instead of paraphrasing comments you said or heard, restate them like you were reliving the experience all over again in the present. For example, you might be inclined to say, *"Fred noticed that there were a lot of pretty women at last week's wine festival."* A more captivating way of expressing this would be to say, *"I was walking around the wine festival with Fred, and he blurted out, 'Steve, would you look at all the hot women here! You and I must have died and gone to Heaven!'"* By replaying the dialogue, you'll be able to capture the original freshness, emotion, and color of a particular moment.

- **Act out the drama with your face and body.** Like a game of charades, a little playacting can give your story some added flavor. By acting out your story with an appropriate assortment of facial expressions, hand gestures, and body movements, you'll allow your audience a chance to see what happened in your story as well as hear it. Don't make the common communication mistake of letting your words do all of the talking. Give your audience a repeat live performance of your story instead of just a bland overview of the content.

- **Reveal your internal dialogue using your own words.** A powerful communication technique used by professional speakers is to express what they're saying or thinking to themselves as another way of capturing an audience's attention. For example, you might describe a moment by simply saying, *"After he humiliated me with his unfair comments, I needed a lot of time to recover."* A more effective way of expressing this same incident is to say, *"I was walking around in a daze thinking to myself, 'I can't freaking believe the nerve of that guy! Who the heck does he think he is? When I finally recover from this experience, it will be my turn to give him something to chew on. That's what I'll do!'"* By recreating the voice inside yourself for your audience, you can reveal your thinking with the kind of emotional intensity that naturally stimulates a listener's interest.

- **Finish your story in 60 seconds or less.** Your objective in telling a story is to give your audience the short version. If they ask for more, you can fill in the details then or later.

Remember that people's attention spans are short. What you might think is a great story may not be of much interest to that particular audience or at that particular moment. Or what you thought was an intriguing tale gets bogged down in the details when you try to recreate it. In any event, almost everyone will listen to you as long as you are excited about your subject, say it in an interesting manner, and make it brief. Like a good quick-service restaurant, remember to serve your stories fast and fresh. Then be ready to switch roles and let the other person do their share of the talking.

When you tell good stories in an interesting way, you'll have a subtle positive effect on other people. It opens the door for additional discussions with your listeners in the future. Otherwise, a poor display of storytelling will cause people to avoid getting into conversations with you out of their fear of being bored.

IT'S TIME TO SHARE AND TELL WITH A PURPOSE!

Find yourself an audio-recording device and a willing friend for this next exercise. Your task here is to take turns telling each other the favorite stories from your lives. You can prompt each other with questions like: (1) *"Can you think of an especially memorable time in your life when you were really excited about something?"* (2) *"Can you remember a special time in your life when you were really proud of yourself?"* (3) *"Can you recall a specific time in your life when you were really happy about something?"* and (4) *"Can you think of a special moment when you felt deeply in love?"* The key here is to step back into that specific moment in time and retell each story like you were living it all over again for the first time.

In order to do this properly, you'll need to review the pointers that are suggested in this chapter. Remember to cut to the chase, leave out the scene-setting, go right to the action, and add fresh dialogue and colorful animation to your stories. On the first take, keep your stories to about a two-minute maximum in length. Then try to give a more condensed version of each story so that it can be told effectively in about one minute.

> "Story is a sacred visualization,
> a way of echoing experience."
>
> Terry Tempest Williams
> Author of *Pieces of White Shell* (1984)

Remember to have some fun doing this exercise. Then listen to your recordings acknowledging what you did right as well as what can be improved. Becoming aware of your strengths and weaknesses is the first step toward mastering this challenging area of your everyday communication.

THE BOTTOM LINE

Remember that in order to "talk like a winner" in the broadest sense, you must "re-live like a winner" as well. All you have to do is follow a simple and powerful rule: *Tell interesting personal stories.* Once you appreciate the significance of this essential part of successful communication, it's only a matter of playing freely with the ideas, practicing with more defined purpose, and putting it to the test regularly in your own life until it becomes a natural part of you.

Ten

Observe

RECOGNIZE WHEN OTHER PEOPLE AREN'T RESPONDING

"God gave you two eyes, two ears, and one mouth. So you should watch and listen twice as much as you talk."

Lynne Alpern and Esther Blumenfeld
Authors of *Oh, Lord, I Sound Just Like Mama* (1986)

observe: 1. to notice and make distinctions. 2. to be acutely aware of what your five senses take in as feedback from the environment. 3. as it applies to this book, to watch attentively in order to determine if your communication with others is working effectively or not.

You're One More Step Closer To Unleashing The Winner Within!
The quality of your communication is best measured by the quality of the response you receive from other people. One of your primary objectives as a master communicator is to watch your audience closely and be acutely aware of how they're responding to you. That way, you'll know if it's time to adjust your communication in order to achieve your intended purposes.

According to the Vision Council of America, a non-profit trade association, millions of Americans of all ages have uncorrected and potentially harmful vision problems. Some of these problems, such as glaucoma (disease of the optic nerve) or amblyopia (lazy eye), may have no warning signs and can cause permanent vision loss, if left untreated. This is why regular eye examinations are the best way to ensure healthy vision for your future.

One of the things that clear vision allows us to see is how other people are responding to us. It's a keen sensitivity to read our audiences that will let us know if we need to adjust our communication in order to get better results.

Being blind to the responses of other people while we're communicating is the cause of many relationship failures. If you improve your overall awareness of such feedback, you'll take a giant step towards improving your effectiveness in your communication with others.

Keep A Close Eye On Your Audience

Many people are so busy talking that they forget to notice if others are paying any attention to them. I had an encounter with this type of communicator recently.

The occasion was a potluck lunch social sponsored by the condominium complex where I live. Originally I had not planned on attending. However, at the last minute, I thought that it would be a good idea for me to mingle with the other condo owners.

One gentleman who I met there started talking to me about tennis. Evidently, he was a big-time tennis player in his youth and loved to talk about the sport at length. Our condo complex has some beautiful, well-maintained tennis courts, and this guy was hoping to find someone who he could swing a racquet with. Unfortunately for him, I don't play the sport or even find it interesting enough to watch on television since Andre Agassi retired. But this fellow kept talking non-stop for nearly ten minutes about his endeared sport without realizing that he was only getting a half-hearted response from me.

I finally had to excuse myself from the conversation and say that I wanted to go get some food. This seemed like the only polite way of getting out of that one-sided conversation. The rest of my time at this potluck was spent staying clear of the tennis guy in order to avoid getting locked into another boring chat. If only this neighbor had given me a chance to talk more often by pausing and asking me a few questions, I might have been more interested in speaking with him.

Like an entertainer performing in a night club, you want to make sure that you keep a close eye on your audience. That way, you can adjust your communications when there's a need for you to get people to respond more favorably. You don't want your audience to walk out or fall asleep while you're still in the middle of your performance.

RULE #10: RECOGNIZE WHEN OTHERS AREN'T RESPONDING

It's easy to become so engrossed on the talking side of a conversation that we inadvertently forget to monitor the involvement of the other people. Here are some questions that will help you recognize when your audience is either fading away or have already checked out:

- **What do facial expressions of concern signal?** Most of the time, you would assume that a concerned facial expression means that the other person isn't agreeing with you. Still it's also common for this to indicate that they're simply absorbing at a slower rate than the pace at which you're speaking. That concern on their face may signify that you left them behind in your storyline and that you now have to backtrack in order to allow them to catch up with you. This frequently happens when the other person is stuck on the meaning of something you said earlier and has not moved forward since that point. Or you may simply be speaking too rapidly or offering too much information for that individual to follow along at that particular moment.

☺ **What could a lack of eye contact mean?** It's easy to assume that people aren't paying attention or listening when they don't look you in the eyes. That may or may not be true. Since it's commonplace these days to multi-task, a person who isn't looking at you may still be paying enough attention to know what you're saying. Or an absence of eye contact may mean that the other person is preoccupied with a different matter. Another possibility is that making eye contact is something that makes the other party feel uncomfortable because of their personal level of shyness. However, as a general rule, a lack of eye contact is usually not a great sign that you're being tremendously effective in your communication.

☺ **How do you know if you're being too serious?** If you find that the other person appears to be getting uptight, it may mean that your discussion is too solemn for the occasion. This inappropriate subject matter could include discussing your current challenges and other serious personal information with someone you don't know well. You may notice them frowning and taking on closed body posture such as crossed arms. Generally, a lack of positive emotional response when you're talking indicates that you have to find a better topic, need to give them a chance to talk, and/or should spend more time listening.

☺ **When your audience is too silent, what could that signal to you?** Complete silence from your listeners may mean that they want you to end the conversation. Perhaps they think it's rude to interrupt you so the next best thing for them to do is discourage you in this way. There are other

"I hope I'm not boring you."

situations in which quietness is a sign that your audience has been stunned by the discussion and is therefore taking time to figure out what it all means and how to respond. When a silence occurs, be sure to periodically ask, *"Are you still with me?"*

☺ **What generally happens to your audience's attention when you talk too much?** People start losing interest when you speak too much or for too long of a time. Then they either want to participate more in the conversation themselves or wish to end the current discussion of an unwanted topic. When you sense that your audience is losing interest, change the subject and allow the other person to have their fair chance to get some words in.

☺ **What does it mean when people move away from you?** Everyone has a certain comfort level when it comes to their proximity to another person when they converse – some closer and others farther away. Perhaps you have a personal preference of standing too close to others and the people you're talking with feel like you're intruding into their personal space. If the distance that people stand away from you seems to be excessive, then there could be other causes to consider as well. Maybe you have a problem with an unpleasant smelling breath caused by halitosis, cigarette smoke, alcohol, or spicy foods. You might be giving off a disagreeable body odor and a change of deodorants, fresher attire, or a medical check-up may be in order. Another reason for keeping a larger than expected distance from you might be that the sound of your voice is irritating or too loud.

How do you know if your listeners are just being courteous with you? Sometimes your audience will give you the false impression that they're responding well to what you have to say. They appear to pay attention by giving you positive non-verbal feedback and even offer you a compliment. But when your listener quickly changes the topic to something that is completely different, then it might have been more of a case of your listener being polite to you. What they may have been doing was waiting for you to finish so that they could turn to their topic, or they might be acting polite and changing the focus of your talk to avoid a conflict.

When your audience isn't giving you an abundance of both positive verbal and non-verbal signals, it's usually a sign that you've got to adjust your conversation so it's more to their liking. Otherwise, you may continue in the wrong direction, moving away from a mutually enjoyable experience for all the people involved.

HOW DO OTHERS RESPOND TO YOU?

In the next week, make it a task to arrange a comfortable one-on-one conversation with a friend. Maybe you can go out for coffee or have lunch together. During your get-together, plan for at least 20 minutes of light conversation.

During this chat, pay special attention to how the other person is responding to you while you're speaking. Notice their facial expressions (looks of concern, smiles, laughter, etc.) eye contact, and other verbal and non-verbal feedback.

Ask yourself these questions: Are they trying to send you a message by the way they are listening? Could it be that you're talking too much and not listening enough? Are they preoccupied with their own issues or simply distracted by what else is going on around them? If that latest possibility seems to be the case, know that your friend could be so adept at multitasking that they can listen to you perfectly well while scanning their field of vision, drinking a cup of coffee, or eating a meal.

> **"Most conversations are simply monologues delivered in the presence of a witness."**
>
> **Margaret Millar**
> **Author of *The Weak-Eyed Bat* (1942)**

The purpose of this simple exercise is to pay more attention to your audience when you're talking. If you do this effectively, you'll be ready to make a shift whenever someone gives you a clear signal that the direction of your conversation needs to change.

The Bottom Line

Remember that in order to "talk like a winner" in the broadest sense, you must "observe like a winner" as well. All you have to do is follow a simple and powerful rule: *Recognize when others aren't responding to you.* Once you appreciate the significance of this essential part of successful communication, it's only a matter of playing around with the ideas, practicing with greater intention, and testing it on a daily basis in your own life until it becomes a natural habit. Know with confidence that the ability to succeed already is inside of you.

ARE YOU
WITH ME?

Eleven

Adjust

Get your listeners more involved

"With Mrs. Fairford, conversation seemed like a concert and not a solo. She kept drawing in the others, giving each a turn, beating time for them with her smile, and somehow harmonizing and linking together what they said."

Edith Wharton
Author of *The Custom of the Century* (1913)

adjust: 1. to adapt, change, or conform to new conditions. 2. to change so as to match or fit into a particular environment. 3. as it applies to this book, to redirect your approach to a conversation so that your listeners can become more interested and involved.

Congratulations! You're More Than Halfway On Your Journey To Unleashing The Winner Within! *Know at this point that good small talk requires active involvement by all participants. As a master communicator, your job is to adjust your conversations so that every participant has the freedom to talk and listen in relatively equal terms. That way, your interactions can be a balanced, enjoyable experience for everyone involved.*

One of the greatest college football games of all time was played between the Trojans of the University of Southern California (USC) and the Fighting Irish of the University of Notre Dame on November 30, 1974.

In that classic gridiron rivalry, Notre Dame held a 24-6 lead over USC at the halfway point in the game. Coach John McKay of USC is quoted as saying during the halftime break, "Gentlemen, if you block like you should, Anthony Davis (the Trojans' running back) will carry the second-half kickoff back for a score and we'll go on from there. Let's go!!!"

On the ensuring second half kickoff, USC's Anthony Davis ran back the football 102 yards for a touchdown, and so began one of the greatest comebacks of all time. The Trojans went on to score 49 unanswered points in only 17 second-half minutes of play! USC won the game 55-24 and eventually went on that season to win the college football national championship.

In the sport of football, the halftime break provides a chance for teams to make adjustments in their approach to a particular game. During this time, football coaches can go over what worked and what didn't work in the first half of the game. Then in the second half of the football contest, a team that has been performing poorly at the midway point can execute a revised plan based on their adjustments to feedback in order to change the course of the game.

In a similar way, most people will go into a conversation with a basic game plan to achieve a successful outcome. But things can happen during the early phases of the exchange that can create unsatisfactory results. This is where a smart communicator reads the feedback and adjusts their strategy in order to come out ahead by the end of the conversation.

Whether it's a game of football, a conversation with an important business associate, or a serious chat with a dear friend, it's not how you start that matters, but how you end up. Making the proper adjustments along the way helps you achieve your desired outcome, and it's especially important when things get off to a rocky start.

"Are You With Me?"

One of the most popular programs on the Food Network for several years has been *Emeril Live* hosted by Chef Emeril Lagasse. The show is taped in front of a live audience in New

York City and features music played by Doc Gibbs and the Emeril Live Band. The cuisine ranges from Cajun to Asian and well-known chefs (Wolfgang Puck, Paula Deen, etc.) are often featured as guests who cook alongside of Lagasse.

What makes this particular food show so successful is the way Lagasse is able to keep his live audience excited and involved in his cooking demonstrations. He's known for the use of catchy phrases which his audiences seem to love, such as *"Kick it up a notch," "Pork fat rules,"* and his most known phrase *"Bam!"* which he uses when adding spicy seasonings to a dish that he's preparing. In addition, Lagasse is able to keep his audience involved even when he's busy cooking by asking a simple question from time-to-time like *"Are you with me now?"*

As much an entertainer as a world-class chef, Emeril Lagasse has made his show a one-of-a-kind television success. He's done this by knowing how to capture the enthusiasm of his live audiences with tantalizing topics, interesting blends of personalities, and skillful communication.

RULE #11: GET YOUR LISTENERS MORE INVOLVED

The best conversations occur when each person has the freedom to participate fully. On the other hand, the worst interactions often happen because one party monopolizes the discussion and the other person doesn't have much of a chance to join in.

Here are some ways to avoid hogging the talking time by making sure that the other person gets fully involved:

Pause to let others respond. When you speak, make sure that you leave room for others to enter the conversation. By pausing periodically, you'll allow time for your listeners to naturally pose a question or make a comment. If your audience doesn't have anything to say during your pauses, you've either got them totally captivated or else you've probably already lost them.

Make sure your listeners are comfortable. One evening, I ran into an old friend as he was leaving a local grocery store. He was holding two packed bags of food in his arms and seemed to be in a bit of a hurry. I said, "Hello" and started a conversation with him, which then went on a little longer than it should have. After a few remarks were offered from each side, my friend excused himself by saying his family was waiting to have dinner. It dawned on me afterwards that standing in the middle of the parking lot, holding two bags of groceries, and being in a hurry was not exactly the most comfortable situation for conducting an extended conversation. I was reminded by this encounter that it's smarter to leave your longer conversations for a time when everyone can be physically at ease. The rule of thumb is to make the majority of your spontaneous conversations in passing short and sweet.

Ask for their opinion. After making a point or completing a statement, you can quickly follow this up by asking your listeners what they think or feel about the opinion you expressed. For example, I will often frame a question by saying, *"I'm just curious if you have any reactions to* *what I said"* or *"By the way, what's your feedback on this?"* If my statements are clear and simple, I'll just cut to the chase and ask, *"So... what do you think?"* Keep in mind that the less comfortable people are with you, the less feedback that they'll voluntarily offer you in return.

☺ **Check in with your audience periodically.** If you're offering a lot of factual content, it's a smart idea to make sure that your listeners don't get lost along the way. Some questions to ask periodically are: *"Are you with me?" "Do you understand what I'm saying?"* and *"Do you follow me?"* Even an occasional *"Right?"* at the end of a statement will keep your listeners in step with you. Just remember that a confused mind is never persuaded. So if your intentions are to influence people with your ideas, you'll have to make sure that you adjust your talking so that your listeners don't get lost and confused in the details of your talk.

☺ **Change to a more appealing subject.** Sometimes the choice of a particular topic may be a turn-off to your listener. In another situation, you could have already made your essential points and it's time to move on to another subject. The smart adjustment is to discuss something definitely appealing to the person you're talking with. That way, you can get them to participate with more enthusiasm because you'll be talking in terms of what they care about.

☺ **Get the listener to do something.** A little known fact is that by changing a person's body position, you'll be able to break their thinking patterns as well. Rather than just talking and explaining, get the other person to demonstrate something for you. For example, if the opportunity presents itself, I might say, *"Rick, show me some of those hilarious* *facial expressions that you like to use."* Even getting your listener to stand up and stretch after an extended conversation will help shake up things. Or you can get them to shift their eyes and head position by saying, *"Wow! Look over there to your right. Have you ever seen anything more bizarre-looking than that?"* In another common situation, you might be faced with trying to influence an unconvinced listener who has their arms folded across their chest. What you can do in this instance is hand them something to hold onto while you talk. Say, *"Excuse me. Do you mind holding this item for a minute?"* This is an indirect but calculated way of getting another person to change their body position in order to break their pattern of thinking.

Add other people into the conversational mix. Sometimes two people can run out of things of mutual interest to talk about. Or two people may not be completely comfortable with each other and it might take another person to be present in the conversation in order to get things flowing. I've noticed that with men, a livelier conversation naturally occurs when the number of participants is three instead of two. On the other hand, it seems like women are completely comfortable conversing in groups of two. If you find that your conversations tend to run out of steam with a particular individual, then you'll probably get in the habit of making those interactions short ones until you've built a stronger comfort level with each other. Until that point is reached, plan ahead by getting into situations where you can add an additional voice to the conversation.

When you find creative ways to involve your audience (like those mentioned in this chapter), you'll be a more effective communicator. The key is to keep adjusting your approach until you find something that works in any given situation. This means that the most important adjustments will be made when you raise your awareness and choose to increase your own flexibility first.

SEPARATE YOUR SUCCESSES FROM YOUR FAILURES NOW!

Take a moment now and think of two different conversations that you've had with the same person in the past. For the first example, select an interaction that didn't go very well and quickly died out. In the second example, pick a time when a conversation just naturally flowed and both of you played an active role.

For example, last month I ran into an acquaintance who I pulled aside. I shared a brief story with them about me being sick with the flu. That conversation didn't go very well because I only talked about myself and didn't give the other person much room to say anything. What I forgot to do is to say something as simple as *"Have you ever been so sick that you couldn't even get out of bed?"* A question like that may have opened the door for this other person to offer a few comments. Or I should have chosen another subject that would have been more appealing or relevant to both of us.

Last week I ran into this same person and had a better quality conversation about a major professional beach volleyball tournament that's coming to our area. The choice of this topic — much more fun and exciting than me being sick with the flu! — allowed a natural exchange of ideas that we both found interesting and useful.

> "The conversation of two people remembering, if the memory is enjoyable to both, rocks on like music or lovemaking. There is a rhythm and a predictability to it that each anticipates and relishes."
>
> Jessamyn West
> Author of *The State of Stony Lonesome* (1984)

After you've selected your own examples, try to determine the critical differences between the one that went well and the one that didn't. Use the list of ideas from this chapter in order to pinpoint your mistakes so that you can avoid them in your future conversations.

The Bottom Line

Remember that in order to "talk like a winner" in the broadest sense, you must "adjust like a winner" as well. All you have to do is follow a simple and powerful rule: *Get your listeners more involved in your conversation.* Once you know and appreciate the significance of this essential part of successful communication, it's only a matter of playing around with the ideas, adding your own creativity, practicing with greater intention, and putting it to the test on a daily basis in your own life until it becomes an automatic part of you. If you should ever feel discouraged or frustrated on your journey, remember that the natural ability to succeed is already inside of you. Just let it come to you. It's really that easy!

I'M ALL EARS

Twelve

Listen

Become an outstanding audience

"Listening is a magnetic and
strange thing; a creative force.
You can see that when you think how
the friends that really listen to us
are the ones we move toward,
and we want to sit in their radius
as though it did us good,
like ultraviolet rays."

Brenda Ueland
Author of *Strength to Your Sword Arm* (1993)

listen: 1. to make a concerted effort to hear and understand something well. 2. to pay close attention to someone who is speaking. 3. as it applies to this book, to focus your attention on other people when they're talking so that you hear their message while at the same time allowing them to feel validated and more appreciated.

You're One More Step Closer To Unleashing The Winner Within!
Most people don't like to listen as much as they love to talk. One of your primary objectives as a master communicator is to give other people an opportunity to express themselves more fully. The simple act of sincere listening sets the stage for you to be liked, appreciated, and respected in return.

The iPod, Apple Corporation's miniature music player, has gone from an electronic novelty gadget to a lifestyle-changing cultural icon in just a few years. One of the newest versions of the iPod called the Nano is able to hold up to 1000 songs, play for 14 hours between battery charges, and is about the size of a thin candy bar.

If you take a trip to the beach, health club, or shopping mall, you'll probably notice dozens of young people listening intently to their iPods. When it comes to hearing their favorite music, these iPod users are captivated listeners. But when it comes to listening to others while they're speaking, these same iPod listeners might only do so half-heartedly.

If we could all listen to others talk as well as iPod users hear their music, then we would send a message to the people we converse with that they have something valuable to say. In addition, this simple act of listening would naturally fill every person's deep human need to feel important and to be heard or understood.

Give The Gift Of Sincere Listening

Many people possess poor listening habits, and in the world of romantic dating, it appears that men are particularly guilty of this. One woman emailed me the following observations about this subject:

> "Sometimes I'll be on a dinner date with a guy where there are no distractions like television, the telephone, or the computer to interfere with our conversation. But despite this seemingly perfect environment, my date can't seem to have a normal, give-and-take conversation, but rather goes on and on about himself.
>
> Even if a guy IS capable of something that's closer to a dialogue rather than a monologue, I don't find that a lot of men retain what you've talked about, if it has to do with YOU rather than HIM. And I'm not talking about long, involved discussions. I'm talking about sharing pertinent, important facts about my life that have to do with who I am as a regular person.
>
> And just to be clear, I'm not talking about sharing 'big' things, necessarily, although sometimes it is. It's mostly just stuff that's going on in my life. My women friends (even new ones) will often ask me things like, 'Oh, how did that big presentation go that you had last week?' Guys, on the other hand, will be like, 'Uh, what presentation?' If a guy remembers well enough to

> ask me about how something in my life went, it's rare enough, in my humble experience, to be memorable and impressive.
>
> Most of all, I've found that more men than women are bad about paying attention and really caring enough to listen. I'm often struck by what a HUGE difference there is between how well men I date listen to me, versus women I'm getting to know as friends. Are men really THAT clueless about what you call 'sincere listening'?"

My response to this type of comment is that poor listening can have a variety of reasons. Some of the common ones include: (1) being distracted by the television, (2) being preoccupied with pressing problems at home or work, (3) trying to listen while doing something else, (4) thinking that the conversation will be insignificant or trivial, (5) assuming that the message will be boring or too long, (6) thinking that there's nothing of personal value in what the other person is saying, and (7) believing that the other person rarely has anything good to say.

In most situations, poor listening will convey to the speaker that you don't care enough about them. It's this idea of not caring enough and giving the impression that the other person isn't important that's a primary cause for poor quality relationships.

RULE #12: BECOME AN OUTSTANDING AUDIENCE

Most people love to talk, but listening is an entirely different matter. If you want to improve the quality of your relationships, effective listening will require you to focus on the speaker – even when the subject isn't particularly interesting to you or the speakers themselves aren't highly-skilled communicators.

The following points are designed to help you develop better listening habits, which are essential to communication and relationship success:

- **Give the speaker your full attention.** Most people have the ability to drive a car, surf the Internet, read the newspaper, or do household chores while they're conversing on the telephone. But if you find yourself face-to-face with another individual, it's more appropriate to give up your multi-tasking habits in favor of focusing on the conversation at hand. Otherwise, the person who is speaking might easily feel like you're not that interested in what they have to say. So the first step in becoming an outstanding audience is to stop what you're doing so that you can concentrate exclusively on the task of listening.

- **Provide positive verbal and non-verbal feedback to the speaker.** Besides eliminating your poor listening habits, it's equally important to install good listening practices as well. Like any good audience, be sure to remain silent, lean towards the talker, and look them in the eyes while they're speaking. In addition, you can smile, laugh, nod your head, and even interject a few words showing your approval or agreement. Some good examples of supportive things to say would include: *"I'm with you." "I hear you." "That's so true." "You're right on!" "That's a good point you make." "Exactly!" "I totally agree with you."*

🌀 **Stop rehearsing what you're going to say.** We all have the natural tendency to listen long enough to what another person is saying until we essentially "get it." Then we spend the rest of the time while the other person is talking formulating what it is that we want to say. This becomes a comical and all-too-frequent game of "verbal tag" where each person takes their turn speaking, but no one is actually doing any real listening. In order to prevent this from happening, we have to resist the temptation of jumping to conclusions and assuming that we know exactly what the other person means before they're finished with their thoughts. When you're preparing yourself for what you have to say, you're inside your own head instead of remaining in step with the other person's communication.

🌀 **Seek first to understand others instead of wanting yourself to be understood first.** Most people wish others would understand them, but rarely do we ever think first about trying to understand the other person. But by turning this habit around in conversations and understanding the other person first, we can learn what is important to them early in the game. This adjustment will naturally result in conversations that are tailored to the other person's liking and it allows for a better exchange of ideas. By shifting the focus to the other person, we learn more about them while helping the individual feel more appreciated. The other person will also perceive you as being more caring and less self-centered.

🌀 **Don't interrupt other people while they are talking.** When you try to hurry people along in their conversation by either interrupting their flow of thinking or by finishing their sentences, you're guaranteed to cause some annoyance. After all, when it comes to conversation, nothing is more frustrating than trying to talk to someone who doesn't want to listen to you. For most people, this is an innocent habit and not something that they intentionally try to do. So if you can remind yourself before a chat to remain patient and let the other person have an opportunity for full expression, you'll start to see how this improves your standing with them.

Keep your body still and don't fidget. Remind yourself that you're communicating to the other person by the way that you listen. If you're acting in a restless manner, the other person may think that you're either bored with the topic, have something better to do, or want them to finish talking so that you have a chance to speak. By keeping your body still (don't fidget, doodle, turn your head, or keeping looking around), you'll put the speaker at ease and give them the assurance to continue sharing their thoughts and ideas.

Repeat their words back to yourself for better retention. It's one thing to fake like you're a good listener by going through all the external motions. But what people really want is for you to be affected by what they say. One way to do this is to take the extra step of retaining the essences of their message. You can do this by repeating their words back to yourself silently in your mind so that it leaves a stronger impression. That way, you can go back to those imprinted words in your memory and share those thoughts with the speaker. They'll naturally be impressed by how much you remember of their message.

☺ **Anticipate the unexpected when you listen.** Becoming a better listener can also develop naturally when you realize that you never know "who, what, when, or where" will bring a good idea your way. When you go on a lifelong never-ending search for inspiration and information, you'll be surprised by what a great listener and appreciative audience you'll automatically become.

For many people, the journey to becoming a successful communicator involves a major shift towards conscious listening and away from excessive talking. By focusing more on the listening role, this type of speaker will learn more about the other person as well as give them the well-received gift of attention. And if you've always thought of yourself as a good listener, you've undoubtedly discovered some new ways to become even better through this chapter.

LEARN FROM YOUR OWN EXAMPLES!

Take a moment now and think of a person who you regard as being a great listener. This is usually someone who you love to talk to because they care a lot about you and make conversation a mutually enjoyable experience. When you think of this great listener, what characteristics or skills (gives full attention to the speaker, asks intelligent questions, is agreeable, offers helpful ideas, etc.) do they naturally display in your conversations?

Now think of someone who you regard as being a generally poor listener. In contrast to the person in the paragraph above, what characteristics or lack of skills (doesn't give any positive feedback, interrupts the speaker in order to talk themselves, corrects the speaker's mistakes or is otherwise judgmental, questions the intentions of the person talking, starts an argument, etc.) do they frequently show when you're in a conversation with them?

With a clear contrast between these real personal examples from your own life, resolve to take one definitive positive action in your next conversation. When you finish that next chat, make a special note to yourself about how it felt to focus more heavily on the listening end. Did you also sense more gratitude from the speaker?

> **"Someone to tell it to is one of the fundamental needs of human beings."**
>
> Miles Franklin
> Author of *Childhood at Brindabella* (1963)

The key point here is that when you trade your poor listening habits for good ones, all of your relationships will benefit. Other people will feel more appreciated by the way you allow them to express themselves more fully.

The Bottom Line

Remember that in order to "talk like a winner" in the broadest sense, you must "listen like a winner" as well. All you have to do is follow a simple and powerful rule: *Become an outstanding audience.* Once you know and understand the significance of this essential part of successful communication, it's only a matter of playing freely with the ideas, practicing with a greater purpose, and testing it every day in your own life until this skill becomes a constructive new habit. Do it in the spirit of a loving adventure and it will all come easy to you.

I'M GETTING SOME GOOD VIBES!!
UPBEAT

Thirteen

Control

Prevent your conversation from turning negative

"Bad quarrels come when two people are wrong. Worse quarrels come when two people are right."

Betty Smith
Author of *Tomorrow Will Be Better* (1948)

control: 1. to direct or regulate a process or outcome. 2. to restrain an action in order to avoid negative consequences. 3. as it applies to this book, the ability to recognize and direct a conversation away from becoming a largely unpleasant experience for everyone involved.

You're One More Step Closer To Unleashing The Winner Within! *We all have had conversations that started off well with good intentions, but ended up badly instead. As a master communicator, it's your responsibility to make sure that you guide your conversations in the productive direction that you intend. If you do this consistently, you'll have a better chance of keeping all of your interpersonal relationships on positive ground.*

The television "clicker" is a remote control device with an array of buttons for adjusting various settings including channel selection, sound volume, auxiliary input options, and color monitor display. Much to the chagrin of many women today, men seem to have an unexplainable obsession with controlling the use of the television remote. It seems like the vast majority of men change TV channels with such frequency that they never let go of the clicker for more than a minute or two.

This phenomenon is so common in the American culture that I even heard a joke about it the other day that went something like this:

A sales clerk at Nordstrom asked a woman shopper "Will you be paying for these items with cash or a credit card?"

While the shopper was fumbling to find the wallet in her purse, the sales clerk noticed a television remote control device sticking out of the top of the woman's bag.

The puzzled saleswoman jokingly asked the shopper, "So, do you always carry around your television clicker in your purse?"

"No I don't," the shopper replied, "but my husband refused to come shopping with me today so I figured this was about the cruelest thing I could do to him."

Like someone using a television clicker, a master communicator will find it necessary at times to take control when things aren't turning out the way that they envisioned. The proper action by the communicator may involve "changing the station" – by which I mean changing the subject matter to a more pleasant topic. Or it could involve "lowering the volume and adjusting the tone" in order to take away some of the negative emotional intensity that may start creeping into an otherwise well-intended interaction.

A smart approach for everyday communication is to let good conversations run their natural course. At the same time, you'll want to be ready to take immediate control before a destructive turn takes hold. Be aware that there's a lot at stake. Sometimes it only takes one unpleasant experience during a conversation to ruin a long-standing personal or professional relationship for good.

LOSING CONTROL CAN BE COSTLY

In November 2006, former *Seinfeld* star Michael Richards unleashed an angry verbal barrage during a stand-up comedy routine at the Laugh Factory in Hollywood, California. His out-of-control rant, during which he repeatedly used the dreaded "N word," was triggered by two black African-American hecklers who interrupted his comedy act by shouting at Richards that he wasn't funny. A videotape of the incident that was still on the Internet at the time of this writing also shows Richards saying to the hecklers, "Shut up! Fifty years ago we'd have you upside down with a (expletive) fork up your (expletive)." On the video, Richards continues to pace the stage taunting the two men with racial slurs and profanity for more than two minutes.

Eventually, someone in the audience called out, "It's not funny," as people were leaving the room. Richards soon exited the stage.

Two days later, Michael Richards made a satellite television appearance on *Late Show with David Letterman.* On that show, he apologized profusely for his racial tirade by saying, "For me to be at a comedy club and flip out and say this crap, I'm deeply, deeply sorry."

In the following week, Richards also hired a noted public relations expert with deep contacts in the black community. With calls to such African-American leaders as the Reverends Jesse Jackson and Al Sharpton, Richards wished to address the larger issue of hatred and racism and to offer his sincere apologies for his embarrassing public behavior. Despite Richards' apologies and extensive public relations efforts, veteran Hollywood publicist Michael Levine, whose clients have included comedians George Carlin, Rodney Dangerfield, and Sam Kinison, said, "I've never seen anything like this in my life. I think it's a career ruiner for him... It's going to be a long road back for him, if at all."

What started out as an opportunity to be funny and entertain an audience turned into a public humiliation and possible career-ending event for Michael Richards. In the eyes of many people, the beloved *Seinfeld* character of Cosmo Kramer and the actor who portrayed him will never be quite the same.

The lesson to remember here is that one conversation that turns the wrong way can ruin an important relationship, a fine reputation, and in the case of actor/comedian Michael Richards, an entire lifetime's worth of dedication, hard work, and goodwill.

Rule #13: Prevent Your Conversation From Turning Negative

If you're not careful, a friendly conversation can quickly evolve into a verbal exchange that nobody enjoys participating in. The following suggestions will help you prevent this from happening in your important relationships:

- **Avoid persistent complaining and criticizing.** We all do some complaining and criticizing from time to time. It's just part of being real. But what you want to avoid is the bad habit of going into a negative mode too often or for too long of a time. When you do find yourself indulging in some occasional complaining or criticizing, make sure that you don't dwell on it too long and mix in some more positive comments in order to balance out your conversational tone. Otherwise, a strong dose of negative comments will start creating a negative emotional drain on your social interaction.

☺ **Admit your own weaknesses up front.** Before you take a blast at what others say or do, it's almost always a smart idea to admit your own mistakes as well. If you come on too harshly in the beginning of a conversation, it's only natural for other people to react with a "Who are you to talk?" type of comment. A good way to preface a critical remark is to say something like: *"Not that I'm perfect or anything close but..."* By using this simple strategy, you'll naturally lower the negative intensity of your remarks so that the conversation won't drift too far away from the mutually pleasurable experience that was intended.

☺ **Seek agreement and then change the subject.** One of the smartest things to do in any conversation is to validate what the other person is saying, no matter how negative it is, by simply agreeing. That puts an end to the other person's motive of trying to convince you. Then you quickly lead them in another direction by changing the subject to something less emotionally draining or, even better, something that's fun and exciting for both of you to talk about.

☺ **Interrupt a negative talk with a surprise physical movement.** In advanced communication studies, this technique is called a "pattern interrupt." What you're trying to do is get the other person to change their body position and thereby interrupt their conversational flow. What I'm suggesting here is that you use your creativity to get the other person to move in some way. For instance, if you're walking down a busy street with another person who is spewing out excessive negative comments, you can ask them to stop talking so the two of you can get out of the way of oncoming foot traffic. Or you could have the other person move so that the glare of the sun isn't in your eyes. The idea is to stop the negative flow with a seemingly innocent abrupt diversion and make it difficult for the speaker to get back on the same mental and emotional track.

☺ **Request another time and place for the discussion.** In major league baseball, if there are extremely poor playing conditions like rain or snow, the game is postponed or cancelled. You can do a similar thing in your conversations by delaying or rescheduling a conversation for another time when it might be more suitable for each participant. You can do this quickly by saying something like: *"Could we talk about this in about 10 minutes? I just remembered that I have to call a friend of mine back on something that's important."* By the time you resume your conversation, the negative emotional intensity may have subsided and you have a chance to end that topic and go in another direction.

☺ **Find something amusing about the topic.** Be careful with this one because you don't want to make the other person's comments seem trivial. If you find yourself involved in a conversation that's too serious or negative in tone, try saying something like: *"Not to change the subject because I know how important this is to you, but isn't it kind of funny how..."* Or you might put an end to that topic by saying an appropriate, smile-producing phrase like: *"And the rest is history"* or *"Been there, done that."*

- **Stop a negative tone by calling it out quickly.** By identifying a topic as being negative, you might awaken the positive intentions of everyone that is involved in a conversation. For example, you could do this by responding to a topic under discussion with, *"I know that we're not trying to be negative about this, but it's starting to sound that way."* Oftentimes, we don't realize when we're heading in the direction of a negative, energy-draining interaction. This simple type of comment will naturally cause people to shift their focus towards another area where everyone will more likely experience an enjoyable conversation.

By giving each of these suggestions a try, you'll start experiencing greater control of your conversations. You'll find that they're less likely to drift into topics and emotions that you will regret later. If nothing else, be sure that the balance of your conversation is not too heavily weighed on energy-draining negative topics. Otherwise, people may gradually start to avoid talking at any length with you.

FIND A MEANINGFUL EXAMPLE FROM YOUR PAST NOW!

Take a moment at this point and search your memory for a personal example of a well-intended conversation that turned sour. It could have been with a friend, family member, neighbor, co-worker, or business associate. Maybe this conversation occurred in an activity centered around work, leisure, sports, dating, or general socializing. Once you find your personal example, refer back to the suggestions in this chapter and find at least one method that may have prevented your conversation from going in the wrong direction.

Perhaps you'll come up with a few more ideas on your own because there are certainly more than seven ways to handle these types of situations.

For example, one evening I hosted a large dinner party for a tour group that I was leading. One woman in the group showed me a poem that she carried in her wallet that addressed the topics of aging and dying. Even though I thought that the poem was well-written, I didn't think that the topic was appropriate for light dinner conversation. What I chose to do was to agree with this woman that the poem was good and that I would read it to everyone in the group the following day. After explaining my position to her, I quickly changed the subject to something more uplifting as a general dinner topic.

The important point here is to find several options that will work for you and to be able to quickly access these strategies whenever you recognize a potential crisis developing in your conversations.

THE BOTTOM LINE

Remember that in order to "talk like a winner" in the broadest sense, you must "control like a winner" as well. All you have to do is follow a simple and powerful rule: *Prevent your conversations from turning negative.* Once you know and appreciate the significance of this essential part of successful communication, it's only a matter of playing around with the ideas, practicing with a greater sense of purpose, and putting it to the test regularly in your own life until it becomes automatic. The ability to succeed is already inside of you.

SHE'S GREAT!
U. Kohl

Fourteen

Compliment

MAKE OTHER PEOPLE FEEL APPRECIATED

"It is happy for you that you possess the talent of flattering with delicacy. May I ask whether these pleasing attentions proceed from the impulse of the moment, or are the result of previous study."

Jane Austen
Author of *Pride and Prejudice* (1813)

compliment: 1. to give praise or show admiration. 2. to express appreciation as a simple act of courtesy, kindness, or respect. 3. as it applies to this book, to reinforce another person's good feelings about themselves with sincere, person-centered words of appreciation.

You're One More Step Closer To Unleashing The Winner Within!
People love to receive the gift of sincere appreciation. One of your main objectives as a master communicator is to take advantage of everyday opportunities that naturally occur to give other people the praise and recognition that they rightfully deserve. That way, you'll dramatically improve the mood of others during your conversations.

I have a favorite Starbucks Coffee store that is located along the famed Pacific Coast Highway near my home in Huntington Beach, California. Its stand-alone building features a modern architectural design with high ceilings and skylights, large glass windows, and an enclosed outdoor heated patio. This Starbucks outlet is a popular spot for the local beach and boating crowd, which includes actress Sandra Bullock and actor-comedian Jay Mohr who have been spotted there on occasions.

Most of all, I like the friendly crew who work there. The employee who usually stands at the front counter on weekday mornings is named Stephen. When I got there this morning, he greeted me by saying, "Hello, how was your weekend?" Stephen is the most naturally cheerful person working there, and it's a nice way to start off my day with his warm and friendly "hello."

Every Starbucks has a tip jar that people put money in to show their appreciation. But I decided to seek out the manager and tell her how much I like the store that she runs. I said to her, "You've got a good thing going here. There are two other Starbucks in this area which are closer to my home than this one. But I like coming here because it's got a friendlier atmosphere. That guy Stephen does a great job for you. Even the customers seem like they're friendlier here, too."

She replied, "You just made my day! I was actually bracing for a complaint when you first pulled me aside. All of us who work here can tell by the sheer number of customers that we're doing well. But it's rare when someone actually pays us a compliment like this. Thank you."

Whether it's during a visit to Starbucks or in an upcoming conversation, remember that if you have something good to say, be sure to share it. And just as importantly, don't forget to express it with sincere emotion. You never know when you're going to be the one who brightens another person's day by a timely compliment that comes from the heart.

Remember That Only Sincere Compliments Count

One of the best ways to score points with other people is to give sincere compliments. If you're perceived as a warm and honest person, others will more easily accept your compliments. But if it seems like you have something to gain or have a reputation for being manipulative, then most of your compliments will end up being wasted and ineffective.

For example, a friend of mine plays piano in an elegant 5-star restaurant. Recently he told me the following about his experiences with customer compliments versus those he receives in the dating world:

> "The compliment that I treasure the most when I'm working is 'You're the reason we travel thirty-five miles to eat at this restaurant! Your beautiful music and warm personality add so much to our dining experience!' I get that quite a lot and it makes me feel incredible. On the other hand, I discount most compliments that have anything to do with my 'education' or 'intelligence' in dating relationships. I usually perceive them almost as a comment about my dating resume rather than an indicator that the woman I'm with really appreciates my true being. I guess it's the emotion behind the compliment I'm looking for in my work environment or my dating life. Gee. Maybe I should date my customers!"

Giving compliments only seems to strike a nerve when it comes from the heart and not just from the head. If you want to improve the quality of your conversations by reinforcing them with compliments, make sure to give only those that you honestly feel. Otherwise, you may create the reverse effect and have people question your intentions.

RULE #14: MAKE OTHER PEOPLE FEEL APPRECIATED

As a former human relations and effective speaking instructor for Dale Carnegie & Associates, I had the challenging task of complimenting my students after they made two-minute talks in front of our class. During the students' talk, I would search for something in their story that I admired, respected, or liked. By consciously focusing on the good in others, I was able to give a sincere and highly-valued compliment. I would find a positive quality and then back it up with evidence in their performance.

I've found that anyone can give an honest and sincere compliment in their personal and professional lives in the same way that I did as an instructor for the Dale Carnegie organization. The following general guidelines should help you improve your ability to present compliments so that you can begin building stronger relationships in your own life:

- **Give compliments immediately.** If you respond quickly with a sincere compliment, the other person is not likely to feel that you're being premeditated and manipulative. However, when you wait to give a compliment, it can seem forced or out of place. That's why it's important to strike while the iron is hot and to give your compliment before the emotion has long passed.
- **Say it in simple terms.** If your compliment is too complicated, it can sound premeditated or designed to shift the focus away from the recipient and onto you, the giver. If the compliment is too over-the-top, then the receiver may feel uncomfortable with the compliment and doubt its authenticity or suspect your motive. The best thing to do is to find specific evidence that justifies your compliment and to express this in simple words.
- **Find a variety of good things to say.** Look for compliments in either: (1) appearance, (2) actions, (3) possessions, (4) character traits, or (5) sense of style. There are plenty of good things to compliment a person on, if you know where to look. For example, I am especially sensitive to people who appreciate my positive character traits

(honesty, enthusiasm, warmth) or my tastes in possessions (cars, clothes, books, electronic gadgets) and lifestyle (vacations, restaurants, and entertainment choices).

Search for the more unique compliment. The rule of thumb is that the rarer the compliment, the more valuable it will be perceived. In other words, if you want to impact a person with your compliment, make sure that you don't state the obvious. Instead, identify something that is underappreciated or overlooked about them in order to have a more highly valued comment.

Make it a public compliment. If the situation is appropriate, feel free to make your compliment in the presence of other people. This will often have a more powerful effect on the receiver of your compliment than by just showing your appreciation in private. When I'm in a casual situation, I usually mix in a comment like: *"I normally don't say this kind of thing but..."* or *"I'm not trying to be a 'suck up' or anything but...."* I do it this way to guarantee that the compliment is recognized. At the same time, it won't seem like I'm trying to take too much credit for being the one who gives the praise.

Try putting it in writing. Sometimes a hand-written message of support or appreciation on a card or memo may have a powerful, lasting effect on the recipient. You never know how often a person may re-read and re-experience the joy of well-chosen words of kindness in their own privacy. I always keep a file of cards, notes, and emails from people who have complimented me in my dual careers of writing and travel. Sometimes I need to re-read their words whenever I get down or forget about those who I have personally helped along the way.

- **Get credit for passing along good news.** A third-party compliment is when you pass along good news from another source. You do this by telling how other people have been impressed by an individual. By being specific and giving details, you can give the gift of a subtle sincere compliment even if you're not the original source. If anyone should be suspicious about this kind of compliment, it's easy to counter by saying, *"It's not about me at all. I'm actually just the messenger passing along something good."*

- **Accept compliments like a gift.** When another person takes the time and effort to compliment you, don't toss it back in their face. Instead, be a gracious acceptor of the gift by simply making eye contact, smiling, and after a short pause, saying "thank you." Otherwise, you may never receive another compliment from that person again. And in some more refined business and social circles, the inability to accept a compliment graciously is a subtle indicator of low self-esteem or a lack of class.

The greatest benefit to giving compliments is that it starts retraining you to focus on the good things in other people. When you start to change your mental and emotional habits for the better, you start changing your entire life for the better. It will also become a lot easier and more natural for you to give sincere compliments once you've truly become a more sincere person.

"I know, indeed, of nothing more subtly satisfying and cheering than a knowledge of the real good will and appreciation of others. Such happiness does not come with money, nor does it flow from a fine physical state. It cannot be bought. But it is the keenest joy, after all; and the toiler's truest and best reward."

William Dean Howells
American author and literary critic (1837-1920)

PUT YOUR KNOWLEDGE AND HEART INTO ACTION NOW!

We all like to receive compliments. The best way to begin receiving more of them is to jump-start the process by paying tribute to others with greater frequency yourself. Take a moment to write a list of the people who you like, respect, and admire. Beside each name, come up with a specific reason why you feel this way about them. For example, maybe you like their smile, sense of humor, or fresh outlook on life.

Now think of an upcoming time when you might give them the gift of your compliment. Does the thought of this action make you feel awkward or fearful? If so, perhaps you can imagine how good it would feel if someone surprised you with a similar positive comment.

For the next week, commit to making at least one person a day feel better about themselves because of a nice thing that you say about them. Go over the suggestions in this chapter and come up with a few different ways of approaching this so that you can start developing a variety of constructive new habits. While you're doing this, keep in mind that you can't raise the self-esteem of another person without also helping to raise your own in the process!

THE BOTTOM LINE

Remember that in order to "talk like a winner" in the broadest sense, you must "compliment like a winner" as well. All you have to do is follow a simple and powerful rule: *Make other people feel appreciated.* Once you understand the significance of this essential part of successful communication, it's only a matter of experimenting, practicing, and testing it every day in your own life until it becomes a natural habit.

I LOVE THESE QUESTIONS!

Fifteen

Ask

POSE QUESTIONS THAT HELP INCREASE THE FLOW

"The way a question is asked limits and disposes the ways in which any answer to it – right or wrong – may be given."

Susanne K. Langer
Author of *Philosophy of a New Key* (1942)

ask: 1. to pose a question to someone. 2. to seek additional information, find more clarity, or to make a request for something. 3. as it applies to this book, to redirect the flow of a conversation into areas that can be more interesting or enjoyable for everyone involved.

You're Another Step Closer To Unleashing The Winner Within! *Asking questions is a normal part of any extended conversation in your personal and professional life. Your job as a master communicator is to ask questions that elicit positive responses from the people you interact with. That way, you'll be able to show sincere interest while creatively maintaining the flow of a conversation for the enjoyment of all.*

Last summer, I watched a new adventure-reality television series on NBC called *Treasure Hunters.* This fast-paced show featured multi-player teams that tried to outrace each other in their quest of a promised hidden treasure. The teams traveled to historically significant locations around the world (London, Paris, Mount Rushmore, Boston, New York, Philadelphia, and Charleston, South Carolina) where they deciphered cryptic codes and puzzles, looking for clues which would lead them closer to solving the ultimate puzzle and obtaining the coveted grand prize.

In order to solve many of the puzzles for *Treasure Hunters,* the teams were allowed to use their laptop computers to access *Ask.com* (this site was formerly *AskJeeves.com,* which featured a butler named Mr. Jeeves). Using the unique *Ask.com* website and search engine, a user poses a question and receives an answer in the form of relevant links. For example, in one episode, it was necessary to know the present-day location of the "Franklin State." The teams entered the question, "Where is the Franklin State?" at *Ask.com* and received answers that pointed to the "Lost State of Franklin" located in what is now Eastern Tennessee.

Questions will naturally occur in any conversation where interested parties are there to share information and ideas. But in a normal everyday exchange, excessive or inappropriate curiosity can be viewed as being intrusive or annoying. If you break rapport and receive an unfriendly reply from another person, it's probably because you asked an unwelcome question at an inopportune time. When it fits, you might want to pose your questions to an emotionally-neutral search engine like *Ask.com.* Otherwise, some questions you ask can annoy people instead of getting them into the flow of a good conversation.

Questions Control The Focus

If you ask someone who's in an angry state-of-mind about a sensitive area, don't be surprised if they say to you, "Don't you go there!" Interestingly, this is what questions do. Questions control the focus of what you're talking about. In a sense, asking a question is like choosing a direction for your conversation. A respectful, intelligent question will usually get a corresponding answer. But a rude, stupid, or insensitive question will receive largely negative responses and possibly damage any kind of developing relationship.

For example, one situation where single women occasionally receive inappropriate questions is in the area of online dating. Initially, the communication between people using this venue is either done over the computer or by telephone rather than face-to-face. For whatever reason, people (especially men!) who meet through online dating can be blunter and less patient about gathering personal information with inappropriate questioning than they would in a normally occurring relationship.

One woman wrote to me with this interesting example of the type of inappropriate questions she's dealt with during her online dating experiences:

> "I was talking on the phone with a guy who I met through an online dating service and he asked me, 'So, what do you do?' So silly me, thinking he was asking again what I do for a living said, 'I'm a human resource manager.' To my surprise, he said, 'No, I mean what do you DO for men? I need a very passionate and sexy woman.'
>
> "So I'm thinking to myself, 'What kind of creep am I dealing with here?' I respond to this guy by saying, 'Well, you're never going to find that one out, Buddy! It is rude and offensive to ask that kind of question to someone you've just met.'
>
> "And then I hung up!
>
> "Maybe the guys who say these kinds of things think they are being playful or sexy, but in fact, they are being disrespectful and tasteless. Sometimes I can't even believe the nerve of some people. Or maybe this online dating thing just brings out the weirdos."

Whether it's over the computer, on the telephone, or in face-to-face conversations, a dialogue with another person will shift direction and change its focus based a lot on the questions being asked. When it comes your turn to ask a question, be sure that you pose it in a respectful and appropriate manner. That way, you'll be more likely to get a positive response instead of a knee-jerk negative reaction. In addition, when you become proficient at asking questions, you'll be able to convey sincere interest, sharp awareness, and honest appreciation to those you're conversing with.

RULE #15: POSE QUESTIONS THAT HELP INCREASE THE FLOW

Sometimes people get stuck in their conversations and have little or nothing to say. The following suggestions will help you assist other people in finding their conversational flow so that they can have a more enjoyable experience of talking with you.

- **Ask with positive intentions.** Make sure that you're agreeable, kind, and supportive in the way you approach asking questions of others. If you do this, then you'll be sending out the kind of positive energy that people will naturally pick up on. Also, you don't want to make the other person defensive by giving them the impression that what they're talking about is wrong. So get a sense of what direction they'd like to go in and choose to go along with them on their verbal journey as much as you can with your questioning. For example, my friend Larry likes to take an ultra right-wing position on controversial political issues. But instead of challenging him and pointing out the flaws in his position, I simply ask him what the leaders on that side of the issue are saying.

Prompt them to elaborate on their topic. If a person comes to a quick halt in their discussion with you, it could be because they're afraid of boring you. You can take that fear away and give them more freedom to express themselves by simply asking for more content or information. For example, an appropriate question to ask in order to get someone to elaborate more would be: *"That sounds interesting. Could you tell me more about that?"* Or you might want to widen the scope of their topic by asking, *"How else or where else is that true? I'd really like to know."*

Seek clarification of their statements. Sometimes people will speak in broad, general terms. For example, occasionally I've been guilty of making a statement like: "Women love to talk, while men hate to listen." Since I may be afraid of a person's reaction to that statement, I might leave those words hanging without further explanation. But you as a listener could keep on that theme by simply asking, *"How do you mean?"* Asking that type of question gives the speaker permission to talk more about a subject that could have potential interest for both of you.

Ask cleverly for sensitive information. There will be many times when you'll be asking a question in the hopes of expanding a conversation that may get you into sensitive areas. These are areas that many people don't want to talk about unless they feel safe with you. To avoid an instant negative reaction, you can begin by saying, *"I'm just curious. What is it that you hate so much?"* What often happens is that the person will counter with: "Why do you ask?" or "What made you ask such a question?" And the reply that handles this objection is for you to say, *"Oh, don't mind me. I was just being curious."* The key here is to be aware of sensitive areas that might cause a person to be defensive. Then it's a matter of having an acceptable reply if you happen to stir up unwanted initial responses from the people that you ask.

☺ **Handle the "I don't know" rcsponse.** Here's a little verbal trick that I learned from seminars that I took in advanced communication. Whenever you meet resistance to a question that you pose in the form of an "I don't know" response, quickly reply by saying, *"Well, what would you say if you did know?"* or *"That's okay. Just suppose that you did know."* The secret here is to do this in a very "matter-of-fact" way so that it works seamlessly into your conversational style. Try this technique on your friends. I guarantee that you'll be surprised by the instant results that you get, which have a way of keeping conversations flowing and opening up new topics to discuss.

☺ **Present questions to keep them feeling resourceful.** Sometimes you'll need to support the person you're listening to with creative questions like: (1) *"So that was a lot of fun for you?"* (2) *"Did that make you feel proud?"* (3) *"How could you not be excited by that?"* (4) *"That's something you really enjoyed, right?"* or (5) *"You must have really loved that one, didn't you?"* The idea here is to access a person's resourceful emotional states by asking questions that make them focus on being that way. Notice that the key words you accessed with these questions included the positive emotional states of fun, excitement, pride, joy, and love. This is where people find the enthusiasm to talk at their best.

☺ **Pose questions to lift their bad mood.** In the previous pointer, I stated that asking the right question will automatically elicit a certain desired emotion. With this in mind, you'll occasionally find it useful to ask a certain question in an attempt to break a speaker's bad mood or change their focus in a conversation. An example of this would be to say, *"That's not the real you, is it?"* when that person is feeling discouraged, frustrated, or disappointed. You've probably heard the phrase, "Are we having fun yet?" This is often said with a similar purpose of changing people's focus when things *aren't* feeling particularly fun.

By experimenting with new ways to use questions as a communication tool, you can greatly improve your ability to interact effectively. You accomplish this by keeping the conversation flowing in the direction that you both want it to go. That way, you can consistently create an enjoyable experience for everyone involved.

MAKE IT A TASK TO ASK WITH A PURPOSE!

Commit yourself now to having at least one 15 minute face-to-face conversation each day over the next week where your sole purpose is to help the other person get into their conversational flow. Put this task at the top of your "Things To Do List." Then go into this task from the position of being genuinely interested in that person and making them feel important to you. Right before your conversation, re-read the suggestions in the previous section of this chapter so that your options will be fresh in your mind.

Once you've completed your conversation, take a moment to reflect on the effect you had on the conversation by the questions that you asked. Did the other person seem to enjoy the additional interest that you showed? Was the other person more comfortable with you as they began to talk more at length? Did you also find that learning to ask better questions is something that you need to work on a lot more?

> "The wise man doesn't give the right answers,
> he poses the right questions."
>
> Claude Levi-Strauss
> French social anthropologist

Regardless of your outcome with this single encounter, be sure that you come away with the experience of what it feels like to try to use questions as a practical means of steering conversations in positive directions. Also keep in mind that the practice of asking good questions will naturally help you to become a better listener.

THE BOTTOM LINE

Remember that in order to "talk like a winner" in the broadest sense, you must "ask like a winner" as well. All you have to do is follow a simple and powerful rule: *Pose questions that will help increase the conversational flow.* Once you appreciate the significance of this essential part of successful communication, it's only a matter of playing around freely with the ideas, practicing with greater intention, and testing it regularly in your own life until it becomes a natural part of you.

YES! YUP!!
YESSIREEE!
SURE!! OKAY!
YOU BET! YEAH!
RIGHT!
SSIR!
NO!
NO WAY! N
NOT A CHANC

Sixteen

Evaluate

Understand the Underlying Message

"Whenever people in general do not understand, they are always prepared to dislike; the incomprehensible is always the obnoxious."

L.E. Landon
Author of *Romance and Reality* (1831)

evaluate: 1. to decide on a value or significance of something. 2. to ascertain, weigh, or judge a topic or issue. 3. as it applies to this book, to find the most accurate meaning or the intended purpose of another person's communication with you.

You're One More Step Closer To Unleashing The Winner Within!
Sometimes your assessment of a person's body language, voice tones, and words doesn't allow you to fully understand what the talker means or intends. One of your primary objectives as a master communicator is to avoid jumping to inaccurate conclusions and to allow the speaker to reveal the full meaning of their message. That way, you'll be able to respond in ways that will maintain good rapport with others even in the most challenging situations.

In 1997, a popular Japanese film titled *Shall We Dance?* opened in American art-house theaters. Eventually it became one of the top-grossing foreign movies in American cinema history. The film is about a typical Japanese "salaryman" who is searching for a break from his dreary everyday existence. What starts as a romantic fantasy about a dance teacher he saw from his commuter train becomes an actual passion for dancing in his own life. This newly discovered passion changes the salaryman's outlook on life as well as his personal relationships.

The success of this foreign movie inspired a big budget 2004 Hollywood remake starring Richard Gere and Jennifer Lopez. This new American version of *Shall We Dance?* proved to be less well-received than the original Japanese film among critics, but still managed modest commercial success earning over $57 million in the United States.

The huge success of the original Japanese version of *Shall We Dance?* came despite being available only with English subtitles. The essence of the film was effectively communicated to American audiences through the body language and voice tones of the Japanese actors and actresses. While the basic subtitled words helped American viewers understand the background and developments between the characters, it was the non-verbal communication of the actors that made this film such an effective and enjoyable movie.

Understanding a message – whether it's in a foreign film with English subtitles or an everyday conversation in your own life – requires us to pay attention to details and, if necessary, dig deeper for understanding. That way, we can more accurately capture the essential emotion, intention, and meaning of what's being communicated to us.

Don't Jump To Conclusions!

If "jumping to conclusions" were an Olympic event, we all probably know at least one person who could contend for a gold medal. Unfortunately, this is not an award that anyone truly wants to win.

We've all been involved in conversations where some degree of misunderstanding has taken place. These minor or unintentional misunderstandings can be annoying and sometimes funny, but aren't necessarily damaging to a relationship's future.

For example, I had a memorable experience while vacationing in the Ozark Mountains of Northern Arkansas in a quaint little resort town called Eureka Springs. When I purchased a souvenir at a local gift shop, the cashier commented, "My, you speak good English!" In this case, the cashier jumped to the conclusion that I was a foreign tourist who was visiting from Asia instead of what I am – an American-born U.S. citizen with Japanese ancestry. I laughed to myself during the incident because I realized that this cashier was only trying to be nice to me.

On the other hand, there are times when jumping to conclusions can cause hurtful misunderstandings between two people. For example, I had some people drop over to my home for an outdoor barbeque last summer. While I was grilling some chicken on my gas barbeque range, a female guest asked me, "So Steve, how do like the flower arrangement that I brought over for you?"

Since I was preoccupied with the chicken sizzling on the grill, I didn't really know how to react to that question for a couple of reasons: (1) Like a typical man, I can't multi-task very well... cook, think, and talk, and (2) The flowers weren't technically an "arrangement," but just assorted flowers that were placed into a vase. Being a former professional florist for over 13 years, I associated the word "arrangement" to mean a "stylized and shaped presentation of flowers." As I thought the flowers she brought me were really beautiful, I would have responded immediately with an emphatic "yes!" had my guest just asked, "How do you like the flowers?" But I instead gave my guest a puzzled look while saying nothing in terms of an immediate positive response to her question.

The woman reacted angrily. She declared, "Well, if you have to think that hard about it, you must not have been very impressed!" That wasn't the case and I felt bad that she took my silence to mean that. I apologized and explained what I meant and what I didn't intend, but this minor incident became a major hassle to sort out.

The lesson here is to avoid jumping to conclusions by spending extra time if necessary to get to the real reasons for a particular person's behavior. That way, you'll spare each other the unnecessary pain that occurs when you react hastily based on insufficient evidence or false assumptions.

RULE #16: UNDERSTAND THE UNDERLYING MESSAGE

One of the keys to being an excellent communicator is to gain an accurate read on the intentions of other people. Realize that each one of us will have imperfections in our communications with others and that there will be times when you're guilty of sending out unclear and easily misinterpreted messages.

To help you evaluate other people's communication with you more accurately, consider the following points:

- **Gauge each other's stress level.** When human beings are in a stressed emotional state, expect them to be less tolerant, patient, and understanding with you. In addition, their communication may be more hurried and forced than at other times. A tense person might also react to your comments with quick anger, frustration, and disappointment. So before evaluating what a person means by what they say and how they express it, be sure to get an accurate read of how strained they may be at the time.

That way, you can avoid misjudging their intentions and realize that their words and actions will be distorted in proportion to their level of stress.

Give people an opportunity to vent. Sometimes a person just needs a patient, understanding listener who will take the time to hear what they have to say. They may not be looking for someone who will solve their problems or even for a different perspective. What people need most at these times is a chance to share the emotional load of what they're going through. Once they are relieved of this burden, they will more likely be in a better frame of mind to converse in a normal fashion. Your job in this phase of the conversation is simply to give your full attention to the speaker. Also provide positive non-verbal feedback as well as verbal input if it is desired.

Determine how other people perceive an issue's level of significance. What may seem like a minor deal to you may in fact be a major issue for the person that you're talking with. When you're trying to understand the meaning of someone else's communication, it's essential to assess how important the subject at hand is to them. When the significance of an issue is low, there's a lot of room to play around in your conversation. But when the importance is high for the other person, an enlightened communicator will treat the conversation with a greater sense of respect and seriousness.

Don't take things too personally. When people feel comfortable chatting with you, they'll express themselves with a large degree of freedom. The upside is that you'll have a lot more fun and variety in your conversations with them. But the downside is that you'll inevitably experience an occasional unflattering but harmless remark against you. A smart communicator will be prepared for these types of comments and avoid reacting too defensively. Otherwise, people may start anticipating your hyper-sensitivity in future conversations, which can result in cautious, but more limited and less entertaining interactions.

© **Ask for clarification on the meaning of a word or phrase.** People will often have different interpretations of or associations with a particular word or phrase. Rather than jumping to any conclusions, it's much smarter to ask them to clarify their remark. For instance, someone may say to me, "Steve, you're full of old-fashioned advice." It might be easy for me to reply defensively by saying that my information is actually "on the cutting-edge." But that person may have positive intentions when they used the term "old-fashioned." They might have meant that "old-fashioned" is classic, timeless, and wise. What I should do in this case is ask how they are defining "old-fashioned." That's a lot better than assuming that I know what the other person meant and reacting in a defensive manner.

© **Recognize when others are just being polite to you.** Being of Japanese ancestry, I am all-too-familiar with polite behavior. I grew up with a distinct bias towards helping other people "save face." By this I mean that when someone is trying to influence me, I am not inclined to say "no" to them, but will reply with a less-confrontational comment like "That would be difficult." And of course, this type of behavior is not just a tendency for some of us of Japanese decent. Many people will comply at times to a request by saying "yes" with their words, but signaling "no" with their facial expressions. Here's another example of polite behavior that I know I do on occasion. I have a friend named Joe who can be really pushy with me at times. I've learned to deal with Joe by saying "yes" whenever he's pressuring me and then to just avoid him after that. This embarrassing behavior is less of a hassle than saying "no" to Joe and having to explain at great length why I can't go along with whatever it is that he's trying to sell me on. In this case, saying "yes" is actually a polite way of preventing an argument, but it's not to be confused with voluntary, enthusiastic compliance.

Don't mistake passion as evidence of truth. Some highly persuasive people like sales professionals, politicians, lawyers, motivational speakers, and religious leaders are skilled at speaking with passion and conviction. But we all must realize that their emotional intensity regarding a subject does not necessarily indicate that what they're saying is true for us as individuals. We mustn't reason to ourselves, "They must be right because they are so passionate on the matter." A wise communicator knows when to separate emotional intensity from the truth because they are separate evaluations to make.

By implementing these ideas, you'll be taking important steps related to making more accurate evaluations about other people's communications. This will place you in a much stronger and wiser position for responding to them in an effective manner.

REMEMBER TO LOOK WISELY BEFORE YOU LEAP!

Think back on a time when you made an obvious mistake of jumping to an inaccurate conclusion. Perhaps it was something that a friend, family member, or co-worker said that triggered an automatic response in you that proved later to be entirely off-base. Did this response of yours cause ill-feelings in the other person? Could this have been avoided if you had taken the time to make a more accurate evaluation of the other person's communication?

Now take a look at the suggestions in this chapter and come up with one or two ways in which you could have handled the situation differently. Maybe you can think of a similar situation that you're likely to face in the near future where being wiser in your evaluations would be important for you.

The point here is to be sure that you do a more thorough job of gathering information before reacting to what other people say or do. If you can master this phase in the communication process, then you'll be able to respond in ways that will enhance – rather than damage – your key personal and professional relationships.

THE BOTTOM LINE

Remember that in order to "talk like a winner" in the broadest sense, you must "evaluate like a winner" as well. All you have to do is follow a simple and powerful rule: *Understand the underlying message.* Once you understand the significance of this essential part of successful communication, it's only a matter of experimenting, practicing, and testing it regularly in your own life until it becomes a new habit.

BRO!!

Seventeen

Align

SEEK THE COMMON GROUND

"Someone has said that it requires less mental effort to condemn than to think."

Emma Goldman
Author of *Anarchism* (1910)

align: 1. to ally with one side of an argument or cause. 2. to create the common grounds for establishing a relationship. 3. as it applies to this book, the ability to create excellent rapport with another person by sharing areas of commonality and avoiding those of difference.

You're Another Step Closer To Unleashing The Winner Within!
Some people have developed a bad habit of trying to prove their own self-worth by disagreeing with others. While this act may add more dimension to a given one-on-one discussion, it also creates the undesired side-effect of upsetting the other person. One of your main objectives as a master communicator is to establish a solid base of rapport at the beginning of every conversation. Once that is accomplished, you can then offer opposing positions and conflicting ideas without risking great harm to an important relationship.

"Mr. Nakamoto, your bill for four Goodrich tires installed and balanced comes to $779.40."

This is what the service manager at a local tire store told me after replacing all of the tires on my 2003 Ford Explorer. He also said that if a wheel alignment had been done several months earlier, I could have driven many more miles on the old tires and saved myself a lot of money.

For those of you who aren't very knowledgeable about car maintenance issues, a wheel alignment is a common repair job that normally costs about $70. In its most basic form, an alignment means adjusting the angles of the wheels so that the vehicle drives straight and true on the road. Its purpose is to maximize the life of a car's tires by preventing uneven wear and tear. As with my Explorer, improper alignment results in unnecessary costs to the owner. In my case, this came to over $700!

In a similar way, skilled communicators will adjust their thinking in order to keep their conversations in alignment. That way, the emotional wear and tear caused by conflicting opinions, statements, and ideas can be reduced and costly damages to important personal and professional relationships can thereby be prevented.

THE FOUR PATTERNS OF ALIGNMENT

There are four categories when it comes to your alignment with others in a conversation. One category called *"sameness only"* occurs when two people are in total agreement with each other. Another grouping is the complete opposite of *"sameness only,"* and it is referred to as *"difference only."* This *"difference only"* alignment occurs when nothing is in agreement at all. In regards to these two alignment distinctions, *"sameness only"* interactions involve little or no conflict, while *"difference only"* interactions will have nothing but conflict associated with them.

The final two groupings are a blend of the previous two patterns and are called *"sameness with exceptions"* and *"difference with exceptions."* Here are the dissimilarities between the two: *"Sameness with exceptions"* occurs when two people agree first with the major topic at hand and then find minor differences. In the case of *"difference with exceptions,"* two people will be at a variance first with the major issue and later discover smaller areas where they do see eye-to-eye.

Being aware of your patterns of relating to others – and in particular choosing the optimal strategy for the proper occasion – will help you bond well with others. In this process, alignment will be a choice. Alignment is about how much you reveal regarding how similar or different you are to someone. But remember that using strategies of "difference" as opposed to using "sameness" is more likely to cause friction than rapport.

WHEN DIFFERENCE LABELED ME A POOR TEAM PLAYER

Several years ago, I served as a seminar trainer for Tony Robbins' nine-day Life Mastery program that was held in Cancun, Mexico. In order to get the trainers emotionally charged to lead the seminar, the Robbins organization had us participate in a two-hour resort scuba diving course. Since I was the only certified scuba diver amongst our group, many of the other 60 trainers looked to me for leadership.

After 45 minutes of lessons in a freshwater swimming pool, the instructors of the diving operation took us out on a boat for a real open-ocean scuba experience. Under less than ideal weather conditions, we hit the water and dove in teams of eight to depths exceeding 50 feet. With choppy seas, limited visibility, and the decision to explore deep underwater caves, this was an especially dangerous exercise for novice scuba divers. I performed the dive in a state of constant anxiety knowing that if anyone panicked in 50 feet of ocean water, we could have a major crisis on our hands. Fortunately for our group, nothing bad happened.

Shortly following this scuba adventure, the leaders of our group gathered all of the trainers together for a meeting to discuss about how we overcame our fears and challenged ourselves. After about a dozen glowing testimonials from other trainers, I couldn't stand what I perceived as nonsense and stood up to voice my strong contrary opinions. To the disappointment of many at this meeting, I said the following:

> "I hate to spoil the party but we shouldn't be celebrating so much. I've been a certified diver for over fifteen years and what we did under those conditions should only have been performed by experienced certified divers. First of all, you should never go on a first open water dive deeper than 30 feet. If you dive deeper than 30 feet, you can get killed by coming up too fast and getting something called the 'bends.' And second of all, you should never go where there are underwater caves in which people can get trapped or disoriented. Someone could have easily panicked and died out there. What we did today was dangerous and unwise. I've got to be frank with you. This incident makes me question a lot about the crazy challenges that we do in this training."

Shortly after my tirade, Michael, the head trainer for the organization, pulled me aside and reprimanded me for my outburst. He told me that I was totally out of line for making my opinions public and that I wasn't supporting the intentions of the organization. I was also told that if I continued to behave in a similar manner that I would be removed from the training and sent home immediately at my own costs.

To this day, I believe that what I said was accurate. But I could have been more tactful in how I said it. I came across as someone who just wanted to stand out by expressing my differences. What I should have done instead is at least agree with the intentions of the scuba adventure and its positive effect on the other trainers. I could have restricted my opposition to the task of scuba diving and shifted the responsibility to the Mexican scuba operators – not the integrity of the Robbins organization. (Note: Anthony Robbins Companies no longer conduct seminars in Mexico.)

This scuba diving experience essentially ended my days as a seminar trainer for the Anthony Robbins organization. But I learned an invaluable lesson about how to communicate strong contrary feelings more effectively in order to preserve the quality of my relationships.

RULE #17: SEEK THE COMMON GROUND

Maintaining consistent rapport with other people is essential to improving your personal and professional relationships. The following ideas will help you align with others even when you're faced with issues where you don't agree:

- **Search for whatever it is that you do agree on.** The simplest way to align yourself with another person is to be agreeable. However, there will be lots of times when you concur on some things but disagree with others. A good way to handle this mixed situation is to focus on the things that you do agree on first. Leave your areas of conflict for another time or after you've already established a solid base of rapport.

- **Point out what you like or enjoy.** While you're interacting with another person, take note of how much you like or enjoy them or the content of their message. One of the basic needs that every human being has is to be liked and accepted by others. You can show appreciation by laughing, smiling, and otherwise demonstrating that you're having a good time with what they're saying. Then follow this up with a comment like *"I really enjoyed the conversation we just had"* or *"You made me laugh with those hilarious stories of yours."*

- **State what you admire in the other person.** As you're listening to someone speak, notice the positive qualities that they naturally project about themselves. You might become aware of their honesty, sensitivity, intelligence, courage, determination, thoughtfulness, generosity, or kindness, to name a few. Once you pick up on a winning quality that truly resonates with you, strike while the iron is hot by making statements like *"I really admire the courage you've shown"* or *"You certainly are a determined individual."*
- **Find something that you respect about their stated position.** You might not agree with another person, but you can respect the opinions that they hold. Usually this act is more a show of politeness than agreement on your part. An example of this would be to say: *"I respect your line of reasoning because it makes perfect sense for you."* For many people, a show of respect can be just as valuable to them as having someone agree with their position.
- **Tell them that you understand how they feel.** "I feel your pain" is a common phrase that people say to express empathy towards another person. Sometimes an individual just wants someone to listen to them so that they can vent and share their emotional load. When people feel truly understood, it creates a subtle but strong relationship bond. This is even truer when the emotion being shared is especially painful or overwhelming.

- **Link yourself at a higher level.** If you find yourself disagreeing with another person over a minor issue, attempt to find the greater objective or higher purpose that you're both trying to achieve. For example, you might have someone who says to you, "Men are such liars!" You can agree with this comment at a higher level by replying, *"Yes, there are people who are definitely liars."* You can also align on a common purpose by saying something like *"You can't build a quality relationship when there isn't any trust."*
- **Reduce your use of the word "but."** The word "but" is commonly used to negate what has been previously mentioned in a statement. For instance, you might say, *"I like your ideas, but I think they are far-fetched."* In this example, what may stand out in the other person's mind is the term "far-fetched." If you insist on offering a conflicting opinion like this, try using the word "and" in place of "but." Decide to say, *"I liked your ideas and they may be a bit far-fetched."* By stating it that way, you avoid the negative knee-jerk connotation that can come from saying the word "but."

While you can rarely agree completely with another person, there are still ways to make them feel validated. By learning to align yourself with others, you'll build bridges of communication. This will enable your relationship to continue to grow even when you don't exactly agree on certain issues.

AGREE TO BE MORE AGREEABLE NOW!

During the next week, get yourself into a few conversations with the intention of observing how other people align or conflict with what's being said. Do you notice how agreement and alignment tend to increase the discussion's flow, while conflict tends to stop or change the course of a conversation?

For a stretch, try aligning with other people by occasionally beginning your response to conversation topics with a phrase like: *"I agree," "I like," "I admire," "I respect,"* or *"I understand."* Observe how others react to this choice of wording. Is it mostly a positive and encouraging reaction? Do they appear to like it when you agree or align with them?

In addition, take special notice of how other people as well as yourself use the word "but" to negate a positive statement. Is this something that you habitually do? When the opportunity arises, try using the word "and" in the place of "but" in your conversations and notice the more favorable responses that you get from others.

The important thing to gain from these alignment exercises is a stretch of your communication skills. This will help you steer your conversations in the direction of your desired outcomes. Conversely, if you're not careful, a steady habit of conflicting with others will become a primary cause of relationship problems and failures.

The Bottom Line

Remember that in order to "talk like a winner" in the broadest sense, you must "align like a winner" as well. All you have to do is follow a simple and powerful rule: *Seek the common ground.* Once you appreciate the significance of this essential part of successful communication, it's only a matter of experimenting with the ideas, practicing with a greater sense of purpose, and putting it to the test regularly in your own life until it becomes a constructive new habit.

YOU'RE RIGHT
PAUSE
I AGREE
GIVE A COMPLIMENT
I'M SORRY
MAYBE
NO COMMENT
YES
ASK A QUESTION

Eighteen

Respond

CHOOSE AN APPROPRIATE REPLY

"Real charity and a real ability never to condemn – the one real virtue – are so often the result of a waking experience that gives a glimpse of what lies beneath things."

Ivy Compton-Burnett
English writer (1884-1969)

respond: 1. to make a reply or answer. 2. to act in return or to react to what another person says or does. 3. as it applies to this book, to make an appropriate, intelligent, positive, courteous, or favorable reply to whatever someone else may communicate to you.

You're One More Step Closer To Unleashing The Winner Within! *Taking time to collect your thoughts before replying is often a smart move to make in your conversations. This gives you the opportunity to choose between responding wisely rather than reacting impulsively to what other people say to you. That way, you can do your part to maintain rapport in your conversations with others even when things become challenging.*

The World Poker Tour® is a series of live poker tournaments featuring the top amateur and professional card-players in the world. The Tour first started airing on American cable television in 2002 and this has led to a boom in poker games at casinos, card rooms, and online gambling sites around the world.

The game of poker is widely regarded as one based not only on skill, but also on *chance.* So it's surprising that the top professional players consistently seem to find their way to the final rounds of the World Poker Tour® tournament. That's because a game of high-stakes poker requires the refined ability to read another player's actions accurately and respond in an intelligent way. That response in the game of poker could be to either fold a poor hand, bet to show strength, or bluff in order to confuse opponents.

Whether you're playing a game of poker or engaging in a lively conversation, it's essential to evaluate another person's contributions and respond in a savvy manner in order to get your desired outcome. In the case of everyday interactions in the "World Conversation Tour," that sought outcome would be to have a pleasurable experience for everyone involved.

WILL YOU REACT OR WILL YOU RESPOND?

In an emergency, we must react quickly and decisively. Here's an example: Let's say that you're a passenger in a friend's car traveling down the highway at 75 miles per hour. After a big curve in the road, you suddenly spot a large object coming up fast ahead on the highway. You immediately react by shouting, "Look out! There's a big object lying there in our lane." Then, as you pass to the left of the debris (which in fact turned out to be someone's king-size mattress), you might say to your friend, "Sorry if I startled you... it was just me reacting to the danger. Good driving! Glad we missed that 'bump' in the road."

In an entirely different situation, you find yourself in a restaurant with the waiter bringing you a T-bone steak. You ordered the steak to be cooked well-done, but you quickly discover that it is closer to rare. You could react at first with anger by saying, "You idiot waiter! I ordered a well-done steak. This thing is definitely rare!" Or you could choose to respond more appropriately by calmly mentioning, *"Excuse me, I think there was a small mix-up on my order."* Then after a brief pause, add, *"I wanted my steak cooked well-done and it looks like this one came out too rare for my tastes. Would you mind having the chef put this back on the grill for a few more minutes? That would be really great. Thanks."*

These scenarios are offered to illustrate the following basic point. When the consequences are small, it's best to choose a more relaxed response to what people say or do. You want to reserve your more intense and serious reactions for real emergencies when the stakes are high and there's little or no time to spare.

RULE #18: CHOOSE AN APPROPRIATE REPLY

The smart habit of choosing to respond wisely instead of reacting impulsively will help you establish and maintain good relationships with others. Here are some pointers on how to master this critical behavior:

- **Pause before replying.** Give yourself a brief moment to collect your thoughts and weigh your emotions before responding to another person's remarks and actions. Pausing is also commonly perceived as a classy gesture. It shows subtle respect for what the other person has to say and makes them feel important in that moment. This is a lot better than jumping into a conversation before the other person has finished speaking because you'd rather talk than listen.

- **Let other people be right the majority of the time.** Another way of looking at this is to stop telling folks that they are wrong. When you question someone, it automatically makes the person feel defensive. The plain fact remains that everyone hates to be corrected or told that they are mistaken. What people really want is to be liked, respected, understood, and listened to *unconditionally*. Now granted, there are bound to be some important issues that bring up opinions completely opposite of yours. But unless it is the right time and place for a rational debate, it may be better to just let it go for the moment. Get in the smart habit of permitting the other person to feel they are right most of the time and you'll do a lot toward building better relationships.

Admit when you're wrong. Sometimes it's hard to swallow your pride and acknowledge that you haven't been right about something. I know this one well. In the past, I was reluctant to own up to my errors and friends even gave me the unflattering nickname of "Mr. Know-It-All." But I learned that a little humility helps us become more reachable to others. If you also apologize for any harm that you've caused, you'll convert some of your worst communication mistakes into an honest display of sincerity which people will naturally find appealing.

Reinforce the other person with a sincere compliment. Giving the gift of a warm, sincere compliment during conversation will naturally raise the self-esteem of the person you're chatting with. This is particularly true if your compliment is specific and backed by evidence. An example of this would be: *"You have a nice sense of taste. Those colors you're wearing go so well with your beautiful blue eyes."* Sometimes people will reject your compliment, but that's more about them than you. Your job is to make sure your message comes spontaneously from the heart. The extra bonus

"The true secret of giving advice is, after you have honestly given it, to be perfectly indifferent whether it is taken or not, and never persist in trying to set people right."

Hannah Whitall Smith
American religious writer (1832-1911)

here for you is that getting into the compliment habit allows you to appreciate what others offer. (There's more on compliments in Chapter 14.)

☺ **Sum up what they said.** When a lot of input is given by someone, it makes sense to spend a moment taking an inventory of what has been discussed. This process allows the speaker to clarify any fuzzy ideas and correct any inaccuracies in your interpretations. The side benefit of summing up a conversation is that it demonstrates that you value what the other person has told you.

☺ **Don't kill their enthusiasm with unsolicited advice.** We all face instances where we're listening to someone talk about their challenges and our gut reaction is to offer our own perspective. But oftentimes, people will have a different interpretation of your motivation for doing that. Perhaps they feel that you're passing judgment or that you're acting superior to them. Maybe it's a situation where the other person merely wants to vent their emotions with a good listener. A wise tactic regarding giving advice is to hold off until it's clear that the other person truly wants feedback. Or you could reach out to them by saying, *"This may be none of my business, but I have an observation from where I'm sitting that you might find valuable if you'd like to hear it."* Either of these tactics is more elegant than bluntly telling other people what's wrong with them or what you think they should do.

☺ **Sometimes it's best to not say anything.** The best response may be no response at all. This is especially true in delicate matters, because saying the wrong things can be costlier than remaining quiet. Recently I saw how silence can be helpful in a family matter. One day, my brother lashed out at me for something that I did to him 20 years ago. Instead of starting an argument, telling him how wrong he was, and making up excuses such as that I didn't do it intentionally, I just shut my mouth and let the moment pass. By not adding more fuel to the fire, I avoided an unnecessary battle and was able to get past a sensitive interaction.

When you choose to respond instead of react, you allow yourself the best opportunity for achieving communication success. All this takes is the awareness and discipline to withhold your initial reaction until you have more time for evaluating the situation. What you'll want to determine is both what the other person means exactly and your most appropriate response.

PUT YOUR KNOWLEDGE INTO PRACTICE NOW!

In one of your next conversations, make it a special point to pause before replying. Take this brief moment to collect your thoughts and evaluate what the other person has said to you. Then make an appropriate reply based on what you think is best for that particular situation. Afterwards, ask yourself if you found that this simple strategy was better than reacting impulsively.

Now select another idea from the list of suggestions in this chapter which you can use in a different conversation. Make this selection a more challenging task or one that you haven't chosen to use in the past. After you've had a chance to try this tactic, evaluate your results by asking yourself the following questions: (1) Can this way of responding be valuable in my life now or in the future? (2) Is this something that I can see myself becoming more effective at with consistent practice? and (3) Would it be worth it to work on improving my responses in order to make all of my personal and professional relationships even better?

> **"If you are patient in one moment of anger, you will escape a hundred days of sorrow."**
>
> Chinese Proverb

The point here is to stretch yourself by learning a variety of different ways to respond in a conversation. When times get difficult or stressful, it's a sign of emotional maturity when you can maintain your poise and behave in a positive manner. It's your ability to remain flexible and resourceful that will serve you well when unexpected adversity takes a hit on your valuable relationships.

The Bottom Line

Remember that in order to "talk like a winner" in the broadest sense, you must "respond like a winner" as well. All you have to do is follow a simple and powerful rule: *Choose an appropriate reply to another person's communication.* Once you know and understand the significance of this essential part of successful communication, it's only a matter of playing around freely with the ideas, practicing with a greater sense of purpose, and putting it to the test regularly in your own life until it becomes a natural habit. If you should ever feel discouraged, remind yourself that the ability to succeed at this already lies within you. Just relax and let it come to you.

WHAT A
STRONG
FINISH!

Nineteen

Finish

END ON A MEMORABLE POSITIVE NOTE

"It was typical of him that he lacked the taste to make a final exit. He spent too long at his farewells, chatting in the doorway, letting in the cold."

Anne Tyler
Author of *Dinner at the Homesick Restaurant* (1982)

finish: 1. to arrive at the conclusion or to attain an objective. 2. to bring to an end, achieve an outcome, or complete a task. 3. as it applies to this book, to complete a conversation in a positive manner so that it leaves a favorable impression on all of those who participate.

You're Another Step Closer To Unleashing The Winner Within! *Sometimes it's not the first impression but the last impression that you make which stands out most with other people. As a master communicator, one of your primary objectives is to finish each of your conversations in a positive way. By doing so, you'll help guarantee a favorable, lasting impression of you and your conversation.*

Sugar Ray Leonard was one of the world's finest boxers in the 1970s and 1980s. An Olympic gold medal winner as an amateur, "Sugar" won championship titles at multiple weights as a pro against such celebrated opponents as Thomas "Hitman" Hearns and Roberto "Hands of Stone" Duran. An eye injury sustained in a title fight against Bruce Finch caused Leonard to announce his early retirement from the sport of boxing in November 1982.

Then, in May 1986, Leonard surprised the sports world by agreeing to fight the seemingly invincible middleweight champion "Marvelous" Marvin Hagler, after a three-and-a-half-year layoff from boxing. The eventual fight in April 1987 at Caesars Palace, Las Vegas was won by Leonard in a highly controversial decision. Many years later, Leonard disclosed the critical strategy that he believes swayed the decision of the fight judges ever-so-slightly in his favor.

The secret winning strategy was for Leonard to finish rounds strongly in order to whip the crowd into a frenzy and thereby leave a positive last impression on the fight judges. He accomplished this by instructing the trainers in his corner to yell out "30 seconds" as each round got down to the final half-minute. Leonard responded to many of these cues with a quick flurry of rabbit punches (rapid, but light and harmless) against Hagler, and Sugar sustained this effort for the final 30 seconds of that 3-minute round. He even went so far as to continue throwing punches illegally after the bell to end the round sounded. Leonard employed this additional controversial tactic to end 5 out of the 12 rounds in his effort to finish strong. This strategy proved to be successful for Leonard as the judges awarded him with the victory in a close decision despite the contrary opinions of the overwhelming majority of professional fight experts.

Whether you're a professional boxer or a person who wants to improve their communication skills, it's important to finish on a positive note. That way, you'll leave a favorable impression on those who may be consciously or unconsciously judging you. When you're dealing with people, it's often not how you start a discussion that matters but how you finally conclude. That's because it's natural for folks to remember their last or more recent impressions of your conversation as much or even more than earlier ones.

GETTING A RAW DEAL AT A SUSHI BAR

Last fall, my girlfriend and I went up to Napa and Sonoma Counties in Northern California to take in the annual wine harvest. After a day of visiting vineyards, an old Spanish mission, a redwood forest, and quaint little wine towns, we stopped for an early dinner at a popular upscale Japanese sushi bar in the Napa Valley.

We sat at the sushi bar next to a woman who was visiting from Mendocino, a lovely coastal city that's 100 miles away from the restaurant. (Mendocino was made famous by the hit TV series *Murder She Wrote.*) The woman at the sushi bar was in the Napa Valley to buy grapes for the wine-making business that she operated in her area. After an interesting 10-minute initial conversation, the woman told us to visit her winery if we should ever be nearby.

After chatting and eating with us at the sushi bar for about another 20 minutes, the woman finished her dinner, paid her bill, and got up to leave. She said an enthusiastic good-bye to all of the sushi chefs and then quickly walked out of the restaurant. I smiled at her as she was leaving, waiting for a chance to say, "It was nice meeting you and we look forward to visiting your winery." But that opportunity never happened as she didn't stop to say her farewells to us or to reinforce her invitation. She did give me her business card earlier in our conversation, but I later chose to throw it away. I also have no intentions of ever visiting her winery. Despite a friendly beginning, one thing sticks out most in my mind. This woman left the sushi bar without the courtesy of saying good-bye to my girlfriend and me.

RULE #19: END ON A MEMORABLE POSITIVE NOTE

Like having a delicious dessert at the end of a fine gourmet meal, it's equally important to finish your conversations in a pleasurable way. The following suggestions will help you develop this important communication habit:

- **Impress others by first being impressed by them.** People waste a lot of time and effort on trying to make an impression. Instead, they should let this process happen naturally by first focusing on what is impressive about the other person. Remember that in the beginning of an interaction, it's only human nature to be more concerned about your own needs. So when you give others the general feeling of being important, it will cause them to reciprocate in kind.
- **Recall your favorite part of the conversation.** At the end, it's a big plus to recall something that you liked, appreciated, or enjoyed during the discussion. Focus more on what the other person did or said than on your own contributions. This is a subtle form of a compliment, and as such, it's most effective when it is specific and personal. If you mention just one or two highlights from a conversation that tickled your fancy, it will usually help produce a lasting favorable impression.
- **Share your pleasant surprises.** Another good way of bringing your conversations to a close is to select something specific that impacted you in a positive way. For example, my cousin Greg, who I hadn't seen in many years, said to me, "I always remembered you as being such an obnoxious little kid. Now I'm really amused by what a

good guy you turned out to be!" When your comment is specific and person-centered, it will have a more powerful effect than simply saying, "It was nice talking to you."

- **Remember to have a graceful exit.** Whenever possible, seek to have a refined way out of the conversation you've been engaged in. This is like being at a party and feeling like leaving early. You can slip out the backdoor and hope that no one will notice. Or you can take the high road by thanking the host and telling party-goers you visited with how good it was to see them. Then you'd smile and wave good-bye to everyone as you headed for the exit. What I do in terms of having a graceful exit in a casual conversation is to say something like *"I really hate to end this conversation because it's been so much fun. But I've really got to get moving along. It's been a pleasure talking with you and I really look forward to doing this again."* Then I smile, look them in the eyes, and shake their hand. I also remember to walk away with an enthusiastic smile on my face until I'm out of the other person's viewing range.

- **Try to leave them laughing.** If you can develop and implement this skill, you'll be head-and-shoulders above others when it comes to exiting on a memorable positive note. The great thing about ending with tasteful humor is that the good feeling sticks with the other person. There is a wise piece of sage advice that goes: "Always leave them laughing." In most cases, this is true, especially when you find yourself engaged in informal social conversations.

- **Express your eagerness for the next time.** Whether you're ending a phone conversation or finishing a lunch date with a friend, remember to comment: "That was fun (or great). Let's do this again soon." It's not enough to simply say, "Until we meet again..." You want to let the other person know that you actually *do* look forward to seeing them again – and that your words are not just a statement of courtesy. Your objective is to convey that there's an open invitation to meet up with you again in the future.

☺ **Remember to finally let them go.** From time to time, I meet with a friend I'll call Jack for a beer at the local sports bar, and he always has an awkward way of saying good-bye to me. Jack will usually continue a conversation with me as he walks to my car. Then he'll let me get into my car and start the engine. But the strange thing is that he'll continue talking to me by starting new topics of discussion like we were still back at the bar. After about three or four excruciating minutes, I have to turn off my engine or else be forced to interrupt Jack and plead for him to let me go. Jack's told me before that he thinks I'm being rude and unfriendly. But for me, his way of saying good-bye is something that I dread and try to avoid as much as possible. Sadly, I've found that in order to avoid this uncomfortable situation and keep our relationship positive, I'll abruptly excuse myself from the sports bar early, say a heartfelt good-bye, and walk briskly to the exit without looking back.

By giving each of these positive suggestions a try, you'll be putting the icing on the cake in your conversations. While first impressions are important, it's also insightful to know that last impressions can have an equal or greater impact in many situations.

"It is the steady and merciless increase of occupations, the augmented speed at which we are always trying to live, the crowding of each day with more work and amusement than it can profitably hold, which has cost us, among other good things, the undisturbed enjoyment of friends. Friendship takes time, and we have no time to give it."

Agnes Repplier
America writer and social critic (1855-1950)

RESOLVE TO ALWAYS FINISH STRONG!

Can you remember a time when you ended an otherwise enjoyable conversation on a sour note? Upon reflection, do you remember having an awkward or mixed feeling about that final interaction?

As I mentioned in the Introduction, I field questions from women on the "Ask Mr. Answer Man" message board that I host for *iVillage.com.* At times, they'll wonder why some men ask for and attain their phone numbers but don't follow through and call them. One possible reason that I offer is that something may have happened between the time the phone number was given and the end of that initial conversation. In other words, a less-than-thrilling ending to a talk, particularly in a dating situation, can easily lead to some ambivalence on the part of one or both of the participants.

The point here is to look at both positive and negative examples in your past where the way that you ended your conversations heavily influenced the future direction of your relationship. Then it's just a matter of resolving to finish your conversations strongly by ending on a positive note each and every time.

THE BOTTOM LINE

Remember that in order to "talk like a winner" in the broadest sense, you must "finish like a winner" as well. All you have to do is follow a simple and powerful rule: *End your conversations on a memorable positive note.* Once you appreciate the significance of this essential part of successful communication, it's only a matter of experimenting, practicing, and testing it every day in your own life until it becomes automatic.

SEEK AND YE SHALL FIND

Twenty

Reflect

FIND VALUE IN EVERY CONVERSATION

"There are many truths of which the full meaning cannot be realized until personal experience has brought it home."

John Stuart Mill
English philosopher (1806-1873)

reflect: 1. to think or ponder over a past experience. 2. to search for the meaning or significance of something that has happened in the past. 3. as it applies to this book, to find the empowering value in every conversation or interaction that you participate in.

You're One More Step Closer To Unleashing The Winner Within!

A wise man once said, "No matter how thin you slice it, there are always two sides." That's true whether it's a piece of bread or the meaning you have for an incident in your life. One of your primary objectives as a master communicator is to search for the empowering meaning of any conversation you engage in. That way, you can learn something of value to use in the future on your journey towards developing better communication and improved relationships.

For four consecutive years – 2003 to 2006 – *The Amazing Race* won the Primetime Emmy Award for Outstanding Reality/Competition Program, and it beat out such notables as CBS's *Survivor*, Fox's *American Idol*, and NBC's *The Apprentice.* In *The Amazing Race,* 10 or more teams compete in a race around the world following clues and instructions to arrive at designated checkpoints. The last team to make it to one of these checkpoints is eliminated from the race. This elimination process continues until one of the final three teams crosses the finish line and captures the coveted cash prize of $1 million.

Each team is composed of two people who have a unique type of relationship with each other. Past examples of team relationships include parent/child, siblings, twins, long-time married couples, high school chums, romantic partners (both heterosexual and homosexual), and couples who are separated or formerly dating. The adversities of traveling and competing under difficult conditions often expose both strengths and weaknesses in these relationships.

When a team is told at a checkpoint that it's being eliminated, Phil Keoghan, the host of the show, poses a question. He asks each of the participants what it meant to be on *The Amazing Race.* In most cases, people will say great things about facing the challenges and how it improved their appreciation of their teammate as a person. But every once in a while, a team will say that they've always had difficulties getting along and being on *The Amazing Race* only brought out more of the worst in them. It's the way that people interact with each other (especially when there is intense friction) that has made *The Amazing Race* one of the few reality shows to grow substantially more popular in subsequent seasons.

Whether you're a participant on *The Amazing Race* or an average person dealing with a wide array of people in challenging everyday situations, it's important to find something of value in the encounters you face. That way, you'll maintain a resourceful learning mindset on your journey toward achieving your goals.

LEARN FROM YOUR OWN ADVERSITY

It's easy to find value in a conversation when it goes your way and becomes an enjoyable experience for everyone involved. The real challenge comes when a conversation turns sour, like one that develops into a heated argument, hurts an individual's feelings, damages long-standing relationships, or questions the kind of person that you are. When this happens, an enlightened communicator must find the good in even the most difficult interaction.

A classic example of a good conversation turned sour involved football legend Joe Namath. In the December 2003 incident, Namath made inappropriate remarks to a female sports reporter during a national televised football contest. When asked by ESPN's sideline reporter Suzy Kolber how he felt about the poor performance of his former team, an inebriated Namath replied, "I want to kiss you. I could care less about a team struggling."

In an exclusive interview that appeared on CBS's news show, *60 Minutes*, Namath commented on this embarrassing incident. He said: "I was under the influence, and when you get under the influence, you may think you have things under control, but it's a fact that you don't."

Namath added that he hated dealing with the painful embarrassment of this incident and felt terrible about its negative affect on his family, friends, and fans. Still he said that he was "glad" that it happened. "It was that incident that brought to light that I needed to do something, absolutely," acknowledged Namath who drank heavily during most of his adult life.

The incident proved to be a catalyst for change and shocked Joe into alcohol rehabilitation. Today, in his sixties, he is sober and leading a healthy lifestyle. A rejuvenated Namath has even stated that after a devastating divorce almost 20 years ago, he feels optimistic about having another chance at love and marriage.

The example of Joe Namath illustrates the following point: *It's not what happens to you in any given conversation that matters, but what you do with what happened.* If you can find empowering value in an otherwise adverse situation, then it can serve as a valuable asset instead of a liability in your life.

RULE #20: FIND VALUE IN EVERY CONVERSATION

You always get an outcome from every experience in life. True, it might not be the result that you want. However, if you're smart, you can find some kind of value in just about anything. The following questions will help you develop the habit of finding deeper value in any conversation – regardless of the initial outcome:

- **What did you do right?** This question presupposes that you did something *correctly* in your communication, and it's up to you to find a nugget or two of value. The mistake that most people make in their evaluations is to only look at the final outcome and not give themselves credit for the small things that were done right. If you look hard enough with compassion for yourself, you'll find something positive to build on in the way you talked, listened, evaluated, or responded. At the very least, your job is to find *one thing* that you did right or didn't do wrong before you close the books on that particular experience.

- **What could you learn from this?** Regardless of the outcome, there's always something that you can learn from an experience. Even if you recognize your mistakes, you'll at least be more aware during similar challenges in the future. The key in this evaluation is to make sure that you can describe a positive learning experience. For example: *"I am pleased that I recognized unfriendly habits that I can definitely correct."* Do this instead of saying, "I hate myself for being such an unfriendly person."

What could you be proud of? At the very least, you can be proud of the fact that you're trying to improve yourself – otherwise, you'd never be reading this book. Sometimes this question will make you realize that you're facing your fears and displaying inner strength. Or it could even be something as small as your willingness to put yourself on the line by engaging in a conversation instead of avoiding contact of any kind. Again, if you seek hard enough with a feeling of certainty, you should have no problem finding at least one thing that you can be proud of.

Where might this lesson be useful in the future? As challenging as this encounter might have been for you, it can be good to know when this type of situation may occur again. Perhaps it was a difficult conversation with a mean-spirited person, and your lesson is to put strict limits on your time with this individual in the future. Or you could recognize that when you're in a terrible state of mind, it's better for you to avoid interacting with other people and instead might go see an uplifting movie by yourself.

What is the truly human side of your personal story? Sometimes it's necessary to experience pain in order to connect with other people on an emotional basis. For instance, we have all suffered from the pain of disappointment or loss, and it can make us appreciate the commonality that we all share as human beings. While positive thinking may have a computer-like aspect to it, make sure that you program a question like this into your memory bank. Using it is a way to keep yourself grounded and in touch with your soul.

What is actually a bit funny about the incident? This question is designed to separate major adversity from minor trivial ones. For example, my friend Fred and I got into a huge argument over a bar bill that we shared during a Monday Night Football game. The place where we went to offered a two-for-one beer special along with discounts on Buffalo Wings, nachos, and fish tacos. After 3 hours of eating and drinking, our total bill came out to only $28. But we squabbled with each other over how much we each should contribute which coincided with a heated debate about who ate more food and drank the greater portion of the beer. A few days later, we both realized how ridiculously cheap we must have looked to our waitress. We're both sure that she'll definitely remember us with a heavy sigh when we go back in there again for another Monday Night Football game this fall.

How could this inspire you? Sometimes a failure in a previous experience will inspire people to do better the next time. Keep in mind that self-improvement of any kind requires a high level of determination. That determination could come from discovering what it is that you're no longer willing to do in your communication with others. Before you correct your communication for the better, it's important that you *stop doing* what it is that you've been doing wrong.

- **How could this experience inspire someone else?** Don't overlook the influence that you might have on another individual through your own example. Perhaps in the past, you haven't demonstrated much in the way of self-confidence or communication expertise. But with your own commitment to mastering the *"Simple Rules"* that are described in this book, you've shown others a greater measure of character, heart, and personal growth by the way you now communicate. This may in turn inspire someone else to follow in your footsteps, maybe even without your prior knowledge.

By asking the right reflective question, you can place your focus on what's of most benefit to you. This discipline will prevent you from experiencing the type of unnecessary and excessive pain that immobilizes people from taking constructive actions. Realize that *whatever happens to you* can be an asset – as long as you have the necessary discipline and skill to convert experiences into life lessons of value.

MAKE SMART REFLECTION A HEALTHY HABIT!

Think of a significant emotional event in your past. This could be something painful like being involved in a car accident, dealing with a deep-seated fear, or facing public humiliation. On the other hand, a significant emotional event could be something that was particularly exciting, fun, or enjoyable for you. The idea here is to pick one incident from your past that was especially memorable for you and to go through the list of questions in this chapter in order to extract its maximum value.

Do the questions help you to put a new positive frame on whatever happened to you? Can you see how the right questions will automatically produce constructive thoughts that will add to your feelings of self-confidence and inner joy?

> "Everything you experience is what constitutes *you* as a human being, but the experience passes away and the person's left. The person is the residue."
>
> Ilke Chase
>
> American writer & actress (1905-1978)

You might keep a bookmark at the page where these questions begin. That way, you could locate them easily. In any case, just remember that they're there for your use, particularly at times when adversity inevitably finds its way to you. By turning to the questions, you'll be able to take whatever happens to you and make it work *for* you instead of *against* you.

THE BOTTOM LINE

Remember that in order to "talk like a winner" in the broadest sense, you must "reflect like a winner" as well. All you have to do is follow a simple and powerful rule: *Find empowering value in every conversation.* Once you know and understand the significance of this essential part of successful communication, it's only a matter of playing around with the ideas, adding your own creativity, practicing with a higher sense of purpose, and putting it to the test regularly in your own life until it becomes a constructive new habit. The best advice I can give you is this: If you will simply fall in love with the idea of you "talking like a winner," this entire learning process will come easy to you.

COMMUNICATOR
OF THE YEAR

Twenty-One

Succeed

Build your reputation one conversation at a time

"Perfection is attained by little and little, and nevertheless it is no little thing itself."

Voltaire
French philosopher (1694-1778)

succeed: 1. to accomplish a desired outcome. 2. to obtain a favorable or intended objective or accomplishment. 3. as it applies to this book, to accumulate a long series of small outcomes that ultimately result in the achievement of major communication and relationship goals.

Congratulations! Here's The Final Step In Your Amazing Journey To Unleashing The Winner Within! *Still, know that creating everyday communication success will not be an overnight accomplishment. Instead, by repeating the basic exercises in this book day in and day out, the sum of your efforts in mastering your communications will automatically add up to the success you desire. This can be compared to achieving a high level of physical fitness. It's only through daily practice that such fitness is realized and maintained, and that's fine. Becoming great at anything in your life is a gradual step-by-step process.*

For 30 years, watching *The Tonight Show Starring Johnny Carson* was a nocturnal ritual for millions of Americans. Carson's quick wit, risqué humor, and natural charm made him one of the most beloved entertainers of his time.

Starting with humble Midwest roots, Johnny Carson paid his dues for success by learning magic tricks as a youngster, working as a ventriloquist, entertaining fellow Navy men during World War II, doing comedy and advertising voicework for radio, hosting TV game shows, and writing jokes for legendary comedian Red Skelton.

During his 30-year run on *The Tonight Show,* Johnny Carson earned six Emmy Awards. In 1987, he was also inducted into the Television Academy Hall of Fame. Surprisingly, after his retirement from *The Tonight Show* in 1992, Carson rarely appeared in public. His closest friends note that he was actually a very shy person. This is in contrast to the public perception of him as the life-of-the-party entertainer we had seen on television for so many years.

When asked about the secret to his tremendous career success, Johnny Carson replied, "My success just evolved from working hard at the business at hand every day." The most popular entertainer in late-night talk show history did not become successful overnight. He earned it gradually by working hard and smart one day at a time.

Whether you're an Emmy-winning entertainer or an average person looking to establish or improve relationships through better communication, the success you create will be the direct result of your cumulative efforts. If you work hard and smart with the purpose of getting better, you can expect to become successful in due time.

ADOPT A "WORK IS LIKE PLAY" ATTITUDE

Most people give up on their journey to reaching true communications mastery. For some, if learning a challenging skill like communication stops being fun and easy, the response is to simply quit and find something else to dabble in. This can be described as the "All Play But No Work Approach" to becoming a master.

Other people will stop trying if the endeavor becomes too frustrating despite their hard work and discipline. Giving up becomes a sensible option when a person strives too hard, because the results don't come close to matching their effort. This can be labeled as the "All Work But No Play Approach" to mastering a skill.

A good example of how people use these two philosophies is in the sport of golf. The "All Play But No Work" player is considered a "hack" at golf. He's the guy (or she's the type of woman) who plays for the fun of the sport and when it starts to get challenging or less pleasurable, this person moves on to a new sport or leisure activity.

The "All Work But No Play" golfer is the type of guy (or woman) who seeks perfection by acquiring the finest quality golf clubs, hiring an expensive personal golf coach, and working seriously at the game in most of the available hours. But somehow this type of player ends up being more frustrated than satisfied with their performance. After a while, this "pusher" type of player burns out on the sport and typically wants nothing to do with it ever again.

> **"It is just the little touches after the average man would quit that make the master's fame."**
>
> Orison Swett Marden
> Author of *How to Succeed* (1896)

The solution to becoming masterful at golf or communications lies somewhere in between being too casual like a "hack" and being too intense like a "pusher." By making the process of becoming better a more joyful work experience, you have the best chance at mastering whatever you choose to do. You have to become a serious student of your activity, while at the same time enjoying the process or journey towards mastery. I call this hybrid approach to mastery the "Work Is Like Play Philosophy."

I must add that the only true failures at golf, communications, and life in general are those who never try or give up too soon. Once you realize this, then you'll begin to find ways to keep yourself in the game so that you can reap the inevitable rewards that only go to those who give important things in life their consistent focus and enthusiastic never-ending commitment.

RULE #21: BUILD YOUR REPUTATION ONE CONVERSATION AT A TIME

Here are some of the best ways to make sure that you build and maintain a winning reputation by the simple way that you communicate effectively with others:

- **Increase your numbers.** One the best ways to improve your communication skills is to increase your number of conversations by meeting lots of people on an ongoing basis. This alone will help you practice your people skills along with forcing you to talk and listen with more regularity. At the very least, make it a task for you to engage in at least one conscious conversation a day. Realize that like any new skill, meeting people may be difficult at first but will become easier with daily practice.

- **Learn from every experience.** Find at least one good thing that you did right in every conversation that you engage in. On the positive side, it could be that you let the other person do their share of the talking or that you began your conversation in a friendly manner. On the negative side, you may recognize that you talk too much or get yourself in arguments too easily. The key here is to make sure that you don't overlook what you do right and to recognize where you can improve the next time.

Embrace the inevitable plateaus. Some people will notice rapid progress in their ability to communicate effectively right away when applying the principles in this book. But regardless of when progress kicks in for you, there will inevitably be eventual periods of no noticeable improvement. These "plateaus" or leveling off periods in your skills are times for investing more faith and perseverance into yourself. They are not times to give up or get stuck in frustration. A plateau is just a reality that we all face in our quest for success. It's a time in which you'll have to rededicate yourself to becoming a true "master" instead of a "hack" in your communications. Realize that the normal path to success in any field of endeavor is more like a staircase than it is a straight ramp pointed upward.

Anticipate your next breakout. The more time that you invest at a "plateau" in your communication skills, the closer you are to a breakout to the upside. Just as sure as the sun rising in the East, an enlightened communicator knows with complete certainty that good things await a serious student who stays committed. In the field of communications, this attitude will equate to more effectiveness in difficult situations, more enjoyment in all your interactions, and a higher sense of true self-confidence.

- **Challenge yourself with tasks.** Make sure that all of your conversations aren't just easy ones. Don't limit yourself to only casual chit-chat with friends. If your goal is to master your communications and expand your range of influence, then you'll have to take on some more challenging conversations. The best way to accomplish this is to make it a specific task to talk to someone who is not part of your typical peer group. Ideally, this would be a person who you respect as having excellent communication skills so that you can pick up some helpful pointers. With this effort, you'll be stretching your abilities by going outside of your comfort zone.
- **Reinforce your positive identity with your thinking.** By now, you've gained a better perspective of what kind of person you're becoming. When things don't turn out quite right, be sure to still reinforce your positive side — through thoughts such as that you're being gutsy, persistent, and tenacious in your pursuit of excellence. On the other hand, when things go well for you, bolster yourself with such affirmations as: *"Yes, I'm an unstoppable person"* or *"I can accomplish anything that I put my mind to achieving."*
- **Celebrate even the small steps that you must take on your journey toward success.** With each success, no matter how small, be sure to reward yourself with special recognition. Perhaps you can do this by sharing your small success with a close friend. Or you could write out your accomplishment on a blank card (like I did after I first appeared on a nationally televised talk show) and post it

on your refrigerator door. The key is to find some outward way of expressing your inner joy. Realize that this is a small but important gesture toward staying committed to your dreams, even if the actual experience may seem a bit trivial on the surface.

Your journey to everyday communication success is achieved by building a winning reputation one conversation at a time. When you show a consistent pattern of excellence in how you talk, listen, evaluate, and respond, other people will become convinced of the kind of outstanding individual you truly are. And from there, it's only human nature for people to spread good words about you to everyone they know. All it takes is the heart and character to make this a top priority in your life now!

REMEMBER TO GIVE THANKS ALONG THE WAY

On your journey to communication excellence, be sure to take a moment now and then to give thanks. Be grateful to the heavens for the opportunity to learn and get better. Thank the people who have supported you in seeking your higher purpose. Give love and forgiveness to those who may have been skeptical of your commitment to communication excellence, but only did so to protect you from the pain of frustration and disappointment.

And last but not least, give thanks to yourself for having the courage and wisdom to make your life better by putting in consistent hard work.

You rock!

The Final Bottom Line

Remember that one of the secrets of lifelong happiness and personal fulfillment is to make your future better and brighter than your past. Therefore, it makes perfect sense for you to invest fully in the pursuit of communication excellence. In the final analysis, your ability to communicate effectively will have a major influence on the degree of success that you achieve and the amount of happiness that you experience in your life.

> "There is no road too long to the man who advances deliberately and without undue haste; there are no honors too distant to the man who prepares himself for them with patience."
>
> Jean De La Bruyere
> French moralist (1645-1696)

Like all things of true value in a person's life, achieving success requires an outstanding attitude with absolutely no negativity, dedication to your clear higher purpose, serious but joyful work, and smart individual choices. But the good news is that in the area of everyday communications, your journey to success is not nearly as complicated, laborious, or mind-boggling as it may have seemed before you picked up this book.

All you have to do is follow a few simple rules... one small enjoyable conversation at a time.

Good luck and God bless.

About the Author

Steve Nakamoto is a former human relations/communications instructor for Dale Carnegie & Associates and NLP personal development trainer for world-renowned motivation and peak-performance expert Anthony Robbins.

Steve has also spent several years as an international tour director taking clients on first-class vacation trips. With more than 200 cruises, Club Med vacations, and escorted vacation tours, the author has had a lot of first-hand experience learning about men and women of all ages, backgrounds, and cultures.

His first book, *Men Are Like Fish: What Every Woman Needs To Know About Catching A Man,* received Honorable Mention recognition in the *Writer's Digest 2000 Non-Fiction Book Awards.* Steve's second book, *Dating Rocks!: The 21 Smartest Moves Women Make For Love,* was a "Best Books Award Finalist" for *USABookNews.com's* 2006 competition. *Dating Rocks!* also received Honorable Mention recognition in the *Writer's Digest 2006 International Book Awards.*

Steve has appeared on over 200 radio and television talk shows including NBC's *The Other Half* starring Dick Clark, Mario Lopez, Dorian Gregory, and Danny Bonaduce. He currently serves as the featured relationship expert on *iVillage.com's* popular "Ask Mr. Answer Man" online discussion board where he offers an honest male perspective on day-to-day issues to women around the world.

Unconscious Rapport Skills

For seven years, I learned and applied many advanced communication techniques serving as a personal development trainer for peak performance expert Anthony Robbins' Mastery University seminars.

What I've surmised is that some unconscious communication techniques are worth trying to master because they are easy and natural to do. However, other methods are extremely difficult to master and make a novice practitioner come across as being either strange or manipulative.

Based on my experience, here are some simple things to do and especially what to avoid when you're trying to connect on the same level with people that you meet in an everyday situation. (Note: Several of the methods below can be used in a more complex way and they are mentioned here for the benefit of those who are already familiar with these types of studies in unconscious communication patterns.)

* Get yourself comfortable first and foremost.
* Match your voice volume and talking speed with the other person.
* Match their keywords, phrases, jargon, and slang words.
* Find the comfort level for the amount of eye contact.
* Find the comfort level for body closeness or amount of space.
* Find the comfortable time-balance between talking and listening.
* Don't break their thinking pattern with a strange or loud laugh.
* Don't break their thinking pattern with radical hand-gestures.
* Don't break their pattern with overly dramatic facial expressions.
* Don't overuse annoying pet phrases like *"Been there, done that."*
* Don't attempt to interpret confusing eye-movement patterns.
* Don't try to match voice textures (nasal tones, strong accents).
* Don't try to persuade with embedded commands or meanings.
* Use tag questions like *"You like me, don't you?"* very sparingly.
* Don't try using physical anchoring (touching) techniques.
* Don't try to match or mirror back breathing patterns.
* Don't overdo mimicking body postures or hand gestures.
* Don't overuse questions in an effort to redirect their focus.

The Bottom Line

Master the easy and natural ways of building rapport and spend the majority of your focus on being a more likeable, receptive, and warm person. That way, the proper credit will go directly to the person you truly are, instead of to a set of manipulative persuasion tricks. Trust that true bonding between people is spiritual and human in nature.

Anger Management Strategies

If you want to be liked and respected by others, the simplest way is to understand and appreciate them first. You will then be in a better position to be appreciated by them in return. To help you maintain a more resourceful state of mind, here are guidelines on how to keep your upsets to a minimum: (If you come from a place of love, this will all be much easier as well.)

IF THE HURTFUL OR PAINFUL ACTION WASN'T INTENTIONAL, THEN YOU ONLY GET TO BE A BIT ANNOYED: People sometimes do or say things that inadvertently hurt another person. Give the person a break because their actions weren't to harm you.

IF THE ACTION WASN'T EXCESSIVE, THEN YOU ONLY GET TO BE SLIGHTLY PEEVED: People may also do or say something a few insignificant times that cause pain. But if they realize the effects of their actions, they will often cut out their unwanted behavior. Give some slack if their painful acts are only occasional in number.

IF THE ACTION WASN'T INAPPROPRIATE, THEN YOU ONLY GET TO FEEL SLIGHTLY BELOW AVERAGE: Sometimes a painful action is merited because it was meant to prevent a greater or more lasting pain. In this case, the action may be warranted because in its proper context it was appropriate performed.

HOWEVER, IF THE HURTFUL ACT WAS ALL THREE (INTENTIONAL, EXCESSIVE, AND INAPPROPRIATE), THEN YOU DO THE FOLLOWING:

1) **FRAME YOUR INTENT IN ADVANCE:** Tell them that in a moment you're going to share something that may hurt short-term, but it is the right thing to do in order to maintain your long-term trust in them.

2) **ASK PERMISSION TO SHARE:** With respect to them, say that you will only share what you mean to say after they've given you permission. Tell them that you don't want to catch them off-guard and make this seem any more painful than it actually is.

3) **WAIT FOR THEIR PERMISSION**: If you receive permission, follow up by asking, *"Are you sure?"* If not, say *"When you're ready, I'm ready."*

4) **STATE YOUR POSITION CLEARLY**: Start by saying *"What you did was unfair to me as a person."* Pause and then state your position clearly and succinctly. Then state what you need from them instead.

5) **STOP THE BATTLE**: If you find yourself starting to drift into the negative, stop immediately and end the conversation by saying, *"All I can say is I'm not angry, I'm just disappointed. I know you're a better person than that."*

* Note: Discipline your disappointment when the stakes are minor, but be strong when the consequences are major. Quality people will come to respect your display of character when the issues matter and will lighten up when they see that you really don't sweat the small stuff.